PONIES
AT THE EDGE
OF THE WORLD

On nature, belonging
and finding home

CATHERINE MUNRO

RIDER

1

Rider, an imprint of Ebury Publishing,
20 Vauxhall Bridge Road,
London SW1V 2SA

Rider is part of the Penguin Random House group of companies
whose addresses can be found at global.penguinrandomhouse.com

Penguin
Random House
UK

First published in Great Britain by Rider in 2022
This edition published in 2023

www.penguin.co.uk

A CIP catalogue record for this book is available from the British Library

ISBN 9781846047275

Printed and bound in Great Britain by Clays Ltd, Elcograf S.p.A.
The authorised representative in the EEA is Penguin Random House Ireland,
Morrison Chambers, 32 Nassau Street, Dublin D02 YH68

Penguin Random House is committed to a sustainable future
for our business, our readers and our planet. This book is made
from Forest Stewardship Council® certified paper.

CONTENTS

INTRODUCTION

*I*T WAS JUST AFTER 11AM *and the sun had barely risen. From its place just above the horizon it cast golden beams of light across the frosty landscape. The stillness of the night had given way to a strong gale from the east, carrying with it lashings of hailstones that periodically obscured the view in opaque, fast-moving curtains.*

I was walking towards the northern tip of the isle. There the sea was visible on three sides. White-tipped waves moved urgently, with little space between them as they splashed against the rocky shore. The cold of the wind hurt my face, so I pulled my scarf closer around me, my gloved hand keeping tight hold of the bucket that the wind kept threatening to rip from my grasp.

Two Shetland ponies, a mare and foal, stood sheltered in the lee of the hill watching my approach.

Despite the storm that raged all around me, there was a sense of peace as I walked towards them. So many must have walked this way, in this weather, carrying feed for their animals. I felt my footsteps join theirs, separated only by time.

The places we live and the landscapes we love are an essential part of who we are. They capture our imagination, stimulate our senses, and become part of our experiences, hopes and dreams. The lives of others, past and present, human and animal, enter our experiences through the traces they leave. A lone rowan tree still standing to protect a croft long gone, a hat on a gatepost, hopeful for its owner's return, or fresh hoofprints by the side of a loch. This book is about these connections between lives and landscapes, place and time.

In 2015 I travelled north to live in Shetland, a windswept archipelago more than 100 miles from the Scottish mainland. I came in search of ponies. The story of Shetland ponies is one of love and survival against the odds. Sharing a latitude with Greenland and with no area of land further than 3 miles from the sea, salt-drenched and windswept, Shetland is a land of extremes. This environment has, over thousands of years, shaped all who live here. For much of history, Shetlanders were entirely dependent on what they could produce from their land. This land was mostly rough, heather-covered hill, exposed to the elements and unsuitable for cultivation.

For thousands of years, ponies have been part of

Shetland lives and landscapes. Living out on the open hill, ponies became smaller, helping them conserve heat. Their winter coat, mane and tail grew thicker, protecting them from the elements, and their agility and intelligence allowed them to efficiently move across the hill in search of food and shelter. Costing little to keep, with incredible strength, despite their small stature, meant they were a lifeline for crofters, transporting people and goods across the countryside and bringing home the peat, the island's only source of fuel.

Much has changed in Shetland since the days ponies brought peat home to the crofts. Ponies are now rarely used as a working animal, and crofting, the small-scale agriculture most common in the Highlands and Islands of Scotland, isn't usually a household's primary economic activity anymore. Yet, the ponies from this time – sometimes named individuals remembered to this day – filled the stories pony breeders told me. Across the hills, ponies graze in herds, as they have done for thousands of years, and people seek to preserve valued historic characteristics in the ponies bred on the islands today. As life on the islands changes, for people and animals, adaption and innovation merge with myth and memory as, together, they continue to belong to these wild landscapes.

Ponies

I watched the line of horses walking slowly, nose to tail, out of the gate and along the tree-lined road. As the clopping of their hoofs receded into the distance, I felt tears of disappointment and frustration spill onto my cheeks.

Weekdays spent trapped in stuffy classrooms — watching dust dance in the shafts of sunlight, dreams of horses distracting me from the teacher's words — were spent longing for this moment, when I had the chance to ride. Every weekend I was here, grooming, mucking out, carrying water, exhausting work in all weather, in the hope of joining a trek when space allowed. But the last ride of the day had just left, without me.

I returned to the stable block and sat with Max, an old, grey Highland pony who'd also been left behind. He stood by me, resting his head on my shoulder. The smell of horse, the feel of his soft nose, and his warm breath filled my senses. I ran my hand along his neck, pulling out the loose hairs that remained from his winter coat, and slowly he moved his head, lightly biting my jacket, grooming me in return.

There was nobody to overhear, so I spoke to him, whispering worries I had never quite known how to put into words. As he listened patiently, our worlds merged, and I felt him understand. As surely as if he had spoken aloud, he told me to be still, that difficult times would pass and things would once again be all right. Reassurance that I badly needed but rarely heard. Perhaps because I didn't know how to ask.

I hadn't realised at the time what a lasting effect my childhood love of horses would have, how these weekends would become part of me, continuing to shape my mind, my body, and the course my life was to take. Every time the wind carries the smell of horse manure baking in the summer sun, I feel a deep sense of happiness, and the sweet smell of grassy breath from soft-whiskered noses brings an instant release of tension. Before my mind has processed the stimulus, my body responds.

If this is the love, built over weekends and summers long ago, then what is the legacy of enduring love? Sustained over generations of shared lives, human and equine, where this love is part of the story of place, entwined in the landscape and carried in the wind. This is the love I discovered in Shetland, where, on the edge of the world, people and ponies make home together.

The wind

I walked, eyes fixed forward, the details of shopfronts and the faces that surrounded me passing unnoticed. Grey concrete surroundings, the never-ceasing sound of traffic, a new day but little change. As I waited to cross a busy road, a sudden gust of wind caught my hair. Anticipating a moment's relief, I turned my face towards the wind, but there was silence. The wind had nothing to say to me. I was separate from it, and it from me. Startled by this thought, I continued to walk, trying to figure out what I even meant by that. What did I expect the wind to have said? And how?

This was my first walk through Glasgow since returning from a week in Shetland, a place whose presence had hit me like a physical force. Walking the island's high cliffs, where the wind carried stories of places unseen, intangible, ephemeral, I felt connected to land, sea and sky, experienced an awakening of senses. Memories, a sense of knowing long forgotten, fleeting, impossible to hold, drifted with the salt-laden air.

Standing in Glasgow's silent wind, I understood that somehow, somewhere, I had drifted, got lost, strayed from the paths and places I loved. I felt Shetland calling me, and in this moment, I began my slow, imperfect journey towards finding home.

My childhood was filled with stories from the north. My maternal grandparents were from Orkney and most of my mum's summers were spent on the islands. She described her deep love of the sea and how, on account of being a woman, her older relatives thought her presence on a boat was unlucky. The days when she, the Jonah, was allowed to join the fishing were some of her happiest memories: days of discovery, with birds overhead and fish below. She always said I was connected to the sea, as she was, and I often wondered if she was right, as I feel most peaceful, most myself, when I am beside the ocean. My dad spent several years in Shetland as a young man working with snowy owls on the island of Fetlar, and I grew up with tales of endless light in summer nights, when great white birds swooped overhead and earnest ornithologists needed to contend with Old White Face, a very opinionated Shetland pony. I visited Shetland when I was three, spending much longer than originally planned due to Mum falling and shattering her knee on the remote island of Papa Stour. While she lay in the Gilbert Bain hospital, I explored the islands with Dad, in a summer filled with seabirds, wildflowers and ancient ruins.

When my husband, Steve, was invited to a wedding in Shetland I was eager to visit the islands again. As soon as we landed at Sumburgh airport I was struck by an incredible feeling of presence, of history, visible in the landscape, alive in conversations of the wind. It felt both familiar and strange, exciting yet peaceful. The wedding was not like any I had attended before, two days filled with celebration that included family, friends and the wider community. I came as an outsider, but was welcomed like a friend. When the week ended and it was time to return to Glasgow I was overwhelmed by an intense sadness and a reluctance to board the plane.

Shetland is considered a place apart, connected to but also separate from the rest of Britain. The islands were originally part of the Norse empire, a time considered by many as a happy and prosperous golden age, central to the formation of a distinct Shetland culture. Relationships with Scotland, though, are somewhat ambiguous. In 1469, the king of Denmark pawned Orkney and Shetland, as he didn't have enough money for his daughter's dowry. The debt was never paid and the islands have remained part of Scotland ever since. Scottish rule was often colonial in nature, with lairds exploiting the land and labour of the islands. Shetlanders' ability to survive this oppression, while maintaining their distinct culture, is still celebrated as an example of an enduring Shetland character.

This Viking identity remains strong today. Norse words and imagery appear everywhere, from the names of streets, houses and boats to the spectacular fire festivals that light up the dark winter nights. Alongside the beards and axes there is a conspicuous absence of tartan and thistles. Such symbols of Scottishness are generally seen as irrelevant in Shetland, symbols of a separate history, and sometimes evidence of unwanted encroachment. When tourist signs were erected across the islands bearing VisitScotland's thistle logo, local residents took it upon themselves to erase the troublesome weed. Today, in a place otherwise absent of graffiti, few signs remain where the thistle image is not obscured by spray paint.

I think again and again about this pull towards Shetland, how a week-long visit left so much of an imprint on me that it changed the course of my life so completely. Shetlanders describe the islands as being a part of them, as being in their blood, and that wherever they go in the world they will always call the islands home. The landscape, animals and history are woven into the very fabric of their being. This was so different from everything I had grown up knowing: my parents and grandparents had always lived a transient lifestyle, residing in areas all over Scotland, rarely staying anywhere for long. When people ask where home is for me, I don't have a ready answer.

Impermanence was a regular part of my childhood. By the time I was eleven I had lived in six houses and changed school three times. Visiting friends' houses I was always amazed by the evidence of years of life within the same walls, furniture made by grandparents, lines depicting children's growth on door frames, traces my family never left.

My feelings about this continual moving, uprooting, are also in flux. At times I have felt a deep longing for permanence and the types of familiarity and security this might offer, and yet, within me there has always been a restlessness – a desire to travel, experience new places – and a fear of being trapped. Yet here I was, living in a city, struggling to find employment other than poorly paid temporary contracts. This wasn't what I had hoped for. I had studied anthropology at university, focusing my work on areas of conversation and conflict between nature conservation and other uses of landscape. I had hoped to continue in this field after graduation, but most jobs required work experience that I didn't have, and student debt and high living costs meant I had to take any employment that was available. The only work I found was low-paid and temporary, which for a time felt OK, but as months became years, I found the situation increasingly difficult. I spent much of my free time volunteering, hoping to improve my CV. Although I was lucky to get a job I enjoyed working for a homelessness charity, this was also temporary, my contract renewed every three months. The relief of each extension soon faded, and even when my contract was extended there could be weeks with no work or pay while paperwork was sorted. I started to feel increasingly anxious and trapped. I couldn't make any plans, there was no guarantee that I could even pay the next month's rent. I was approaching thirty and hoped one day to start a family, but I didn't see how this could ever be possible while I lived with such uncertainty. I felt happiest at weekends when I could leave the city, taking my tent and walking the hills and coastlines, escaping for a time. But that moment in the wind told me this wasn't enough, that something had to change.

Around this time I reread Tim Ingold's *The Perception of the Environment*, in which he states that 'through living in it, the landscape becomes a part of us, just as we are a part of it'. The beauty of this line led to me to read more books about the deeply social and reciprocal bonds humans can have with landscapes and animals. Descriptions of more than human worlds, co-created through everyday relationships, got me thinking about my own changing connections to place. I spent my childhood talking to plants and animals, feeling joy and wonder at the natural world, exploring beaches and forests, and feeling entirely at home, even when the houses I lived in changed. I had not noticed these relationships fading, but over time they had, and nature had become somewhere I visited rather than where I was at home. Had I just grown up, the process of becoming an adult necessitating a shift away from an animate nature? Or had I grown apart from an essential part of who I was? It had been such a gradual process, one I had largely not noticed until I felt the intense connection to Shetland.

As life continued, beneath the usual routine, a plan

started to form. I had always thought I might return to university someday and now I realised I could combine these questions about our relationships with place and my desire to return to Shetland by starting a PhD. I was delighted when my application to the University of Aberdeen was accepted, but I was unable to secure funding that year. I had the choice to defer starting until the following year or begin that first year, working to support myself while applying for funding. I knew I couldn't wait. I handed in my notice to my job and flat, and together with my husband, Steve, moved to Aberdeen to start my PhD. Looking back, deciding to move with no job, no funding and no guarantee of either seems incredibly reckless, but I had an overwhelming sense that it was the right thing to do and that things would, somehow, work out.

I completed coursework and funding applications while working the night shift, feverish with a combination of sleep deprivation and caffeine. My anxiety increased as I had funding applications rejected, saw talented colleagues also missing out on opportunities, and began to realise how difficult it was to secure these few grants. There would be no option to continue without funding: university fees alone are thousands of pounds, and a PhD requires extensive work that would be impossible with the number of hours I would need to work to cover basic living costs and the move to

Shetland. But still, as I walked city streets, feeling the presence of the sea, thinking about Shetland, I felt I was finally on the path I was supposed to be walking.

Thankfully, towards the end of that year, I secured a full studentship for my research proposal on Shetland ponies. When I heard the news I could hardly breathe with gratitude and excitement: not only was my dream of going to Shetland a reality, but this would allow me to, once again, spend my days with horses. My PhD position was with the anthropology department's Arctic Domus project. This multidisciplinary team's remit was to rethink the concept of domestication through studying human–animal relations in northern places.

Domestication has traditionally been understood as a point in history where humans gained control over animals and landscapes. It's often associated with a separation from, and commodification of, nature. While this was once celebrated as evidence of humans' step into civilisation, much in these relationships is now considered harmful. The exploitation and violence of industrial farming wreaks unthinkable harm on animals and ecosystems, reducing biodiversity and accelerating climate change. But these processes are also hurting us, turning nature into resources and profit rather than something to be understood and respected, something to be loved that may be capable of loving us in return. The home I

describe in these pages, belonging created through relationships between people, ponies and landscape in
Shetland, is situated and particular. Yet we all live in an
interconnected world, and so how we all make home
affects the very planet we live on.

If we become who we are through our lives with
others, then silencing so many potential relationships –
those with landscapes and animals – leaves us isolated,
feeling separate from the worlds in which we live,
rather than part of an ongoing, engaged social life. This
is why I want to tell a different story about domestication and home. A home co-created with animals,
based on love, respect and gratitude, where through
their domestication practices Shetland pony breeders
are actively creating possibilities for shared lives. When
Shetland summers are spent outdoors with foals that
will form the next generation of island ponies, and
winter winds simultaneously carry stories of past survival and hopes for unknown futures, then this land
truly becomes part of body and mind. These connections are social and reciprocal. Through their love, their
ways of noticing nature every day, people affect the
land and animals, and feel this love returned through
the landscape, their home.

When we know how to look, listen, notice and
respond to the lives around us, the world we inhabit
becomes a more social and loving place. For the earth,

sea and sky to speak to us, we must know how to listen. How we speak of, and to, land and animals affects our relationships with them, shaping what conversations are possible and transforming the worlds we inhabit. Shetland is not in my blood, there is no place that contains the memory of generations of my family, no roots. Yet as I began my new life on the islands, I began to feel more connected to the worlds around me. I came to realise that home is not just a place, but a journey. Even for those who have found home, who can identify where and what it is, perhaps even trace roots back for generations, the journey home always continues. For home is a relationship, a way of being, an ongoing act of communication and reciprocation. It is created and recreated through living.

Ponies
by Robin Munro, 1973

But you have to come back to Shetland
for the true strain.
They grow weak at the knees in France and in
Suffolk meadows.
They degenerate.

They need the wind all the time
the lift of the scattald, the bare
mouthful of moor
cropped from the stone
tasting of flowers

and a salt whipping, force five 'Viking',
to fairly set them moving.

Like fire, they are not to be stopped.
But unlike fire, they are soon contented
in a different geometry
an unspoiled taste
and a same old world.

1

THE ARRIVAL

I STARED OUT THE WINDSCREEN as wave after wave crashed over the bonnet of my car. All around me the sea rose and swelled; the smells of salt and engine oil seeped into the confines of the car, adding to my nausea. The sound of the boat's engine seemed unnaturally loud, revving and droning, a sound felt as well as heard as it reverberated through my body. As the ferry lurched from side to side, I glanced uneasily at the cars next to me. There was nothing to secure them to the deck, we'd been told just to drive onto the boat, park and apply the handbrake. Waiting at the ferry terminal, when I first caught sight of the *Hendra*, I had hoped that this was not the island ferry. With a dark blue hull, white wheelhouse and bright red smokestack, she seemed so small in the churning sea.

Surrounded by boxes of clothes and books, with much of my seat taken up by the branches of a large pot plant, I wondered what I had got myself into. Steve and I were making our first journey to the island of Whalsay, the place that was to be our new home, and I feared this boat journey – the only way onto or off the island – would take a bit of getting used to. I had never imagined I would move to one of the islands. However, when I'd started looking for houses to rent on the mainland of Shetland, I'd discovered that almost all properties were filled with temporary workers while a new gas pipeline was being constructed. I'd begun to worry, as nowhere that was advertised as for rent was affordable for us to live. Thankfully, a pony breeder I had been chatting to had put me in touch with someone who had a house on Whalsay, and the price I'd been quoted was remarkably reasonable. Having never visited the isle, though, I'd done a quick Google search. I'd learned that Whalsay had a population of around a thousand people, was around 5 miles long, 2 miles wide, and a thirty-minute ferry journey from mainland Shetland. It was easy to see why it was nicknamed 'the Bonnie Isle' as I'd looked at photo after photo of dramatic coastlines and fields filled with wildflowers. Although the ferry service was fairly regular, I knew that being far from many pony studs and working to a ferry timetable would hamper fieldwork spontaneity. However, with no other affordable accommodation available, I'd had to say yes.

The sound of the engine rose to a whine and the water around us started to churn as, with alarming speed, the ferry turned 180 degrees. Simultaneously, the bow began to slowly open, revealing the harbour where we were about to dock. A young man in a high-visibility suit appeared from one of the doors and, braced against the wind, moved quickly towards the front of the boat. Once the ramp attaching boat to harbour was secured, he stood in front of the line of cars. He pointed to the car beside us, who drove swiftly off the boat. Then it was our turn. The bumpy textured metal beneath the wheels changed to smooth concrete. We were back on solid ground. I looked for a place to park the car and recover a little from the journey. The harbour area was larger than I'd expected. Sheltered by the ferry slipway was a marina, where small, colourful boats bobbed in the water. On the other side a large concrete pier extended into the water. Attached by lines of thick rope were the largest fishing boats I had ever seen. Blue, red and yellow, the *Zephyr*, *Serene* and *Charisma*, three multi-million-pound pelagic trawlers owned and operated by island families. The houses around the harbour were arranged higgledy-piggledy extending up the hillside. Sheep grazed in the green spaces between houses, but I couldn't see any people other than the man from the ferry who was standing in the same position, and now signalling to the queue of cars that were driving onto the *Hendra* to make their way to the mainland.

I put the postcode into the satnav, at this point unaware of how utterly useless this device would prove to be in Shetland. Within a minute of driving the houses became further apart, the row of lampposts ended, and the road narrowed. We followed the single-track road as it wound its way across the island, roughly following the line of the shore. The houses we passed were in clusters of four or five. Beyond their garden fences were fields of sheep and large areas of rough hill punctuated by small lochs. Despite being close to midday the sun was low in the sky, casting long shadows across the landscape and giving the impression of sunset. The heather-covered hills were a shifting kaleidoscope of earth shades. Glowing rust reds of sunlit heather flowed into the deep brown of exposed peat, merging with greens and golds of winter grass. With no trees, the sky appeared vast, ever-changing with the strong winds sweeping over land and sea.

'You have reached your destination,' the disembodied voice announced as we came over the brow of a small hill. To our left was a group of houses, scattered along a strip of land between a loch and the sea. I checked the hand-drawn map that our landlord had given us. The sketched outlines of houses included details of their occupants, including names and how everybody in each house was related to one another. It looked like we were in the right place, so I tentatively started towards a pebble-dashed house and knocked on the door. There was no answer. Having been told that the door would be left unlocked for us, I tried the handle and sure enough, the door opened. Inside were rows of wellies and jackets neatly hung on hooks. Realising that I had just walked into a stranger's house, I hastily retreated and, hoping nobody had seen my indiscretion, knocked on the door of the next house. It was answered immediately by a neatly dressed woman.

'You'll be the new folk,' she said. 'You're wanting Margaret and Willie's hoose, just doon tha road.'

As we drove over the crest of a hill, I caught a glimpse of the next small group of houses, nestled between hill, loch and rocky cove: this was the township of Vevoe, the place that would be our new home. Standing outside the house, waiting for our arrival, stood an elderly woman, her back straight against the wind. She welcomed us with a smile and invited us into her house, which was next door to ours. As we sat in her warm kitchen she introduced herself as Ina, our landlord's aunt. She asked us about our journey as her brother, Robbie, with whom she shared a house, joined us.

'Toy?' Ina asked. I'd thought I had prepared myself for the island's dialect, so rich and distinct that it has become somewhat legendary within Shetland and beyond. However, here I was falling at the first hurdle. I must have looked confused because again, louder, she said, 'Toy? Wuid you like a cup o' toy?'

Tea! Of course. I hurriedly said I would love a cup of tea and tried to pay closer attention as she and Robbie spoke. With a little concentration, I found the lilting, musical accent fairly easy to understand, and recognised many of the dialect words from the Shetland dictionary I had read before the move. It was some time later that I realised Ina and Robbie were 'knapping': adjusting the local accent and dialect, to make it easier for us to understand.

Robbie told us that not so long ago, you would know where in this small island somebody came from by their accent. Now, with more regular ferries leading to easier travel across Shetland, these subtle distinctions have been lost. Even so, you can still largely tell the area somebody is from by the words they use. They both listened as we explained what had brought us here. Robbie described some of the horses that had been part of island life, ones out on the hill used to transport peat, and others that made deliveries from the shop. He said a few folk on the isle kept horses for breeding, and the good riders among the children take Shetland ponies south to race. Names of people and places flowed as Robbie and Ina discussed with each other who I would be best to meet to learn more about Shetland's animals.

Outside the warm light began to take on more distinct colours of sunset. 'This is about the darkest time of year,' Robbie said. 'At midsummer, though, you can read a newspaper outside at midnight.' Suddenly realising that it was about to get dark and we had not yet been in our house, we said our goodbyes and went next door to our new home.

I knew that unless they lived in Lerwick, Shetland people rarely locked their front door. Not wanting to seem like outsiders, we had decided to do the same. But out of habit, after we walked through our new front door Steve locked it behind us. Moments later there was a scuffle and a thud. The sound of a visitor, so used to the door being open, stepping forward as they turned the handle and walking straight into the door. Mortified, I rushed to meet them, apologising as I scrabbled with the lock. I worried we were already making a bad impression and it was only our first day. I hastily explained that it was a city habit to lock the door and that we would get into the way of things. Our visitor didn't seem at all perturbed. He laughed and said nobody locked their houses here, and to make sure we never locked our car on the ferry as any bump in the water would set off the alarms and drive everybody mad. He laughed again before adding that people didn't even lock their cars when they had guns in the boot. Laughing along, I could only hope he was joking.

After he left, I explored the house. I was used to the neutral furnishing of rented city flats, and this felt like stepping into somebody's home, as if the true inhabitants were only temporarily absent and could return at any moment. The walls were adorned with intricately patterned paper and the ceilings were covered with textured white wallpaper. Cupboards were filled with floral plates and bowls; Scottish blend tea tins housed a selection of screws, lightbulbs and candles, and a set of baskets in the wardrobe were labelled in black pen: BURRA. Paintings of boats and Shetland landscapes decorated the walls, as well as a large framed photograph of an owl sitting on the living-room sofa. My eye was drawn to a bright green-and-blue scene, which I soon realised was an aerial view of Vevoe, the cluster of houses appearing tiny in the vast expanse of hill and sea. I couldn't quite believe that we were here.

The following morning, as I tried to unpack, I couldn't stay still. Again and again I was drawn to the window to look out on the world of sea and sky. Deciding that practical tasks could wait, I set out walking, desperate to explore my new home. In front of the house was a small garden, bordered by leafless bushes that I assumed were rosa rugosa (I couldn't imagine what else could grow so profusely in such an exposed location). The outlines of what used to be flower beds or vegetable patches were overgrown with a thick carpet of tangled straw-like grass. I followed the path to the end of the garden and out a small wooden gate and walked towards the sea. Just metres from our house was the beach, a crescent of stones, a small inlet in rugged, rocky coastline. A fresh breeze blew, filling the air with a cold that seemed to pierce layers of clothing, chilling my bones. The water was calm and so clear that I could see patterns on the pebbles below, the division between land and sea uncertain and always in motion. Behind me, towards the houses, a bank of larger stones had been built. It was clearly a defence, protecting the houses from the power of waves that today seemed unimaginable.

On one side of the beach was an area of rough, heathery ground, which appeared empty except for a few sheep, widely scattered across the landscape. But as I got closer, I saw there were far more sheep than I had realised. Their colours, shades of brown, gold, grey and black, blended perfectly with the hillside. They seemed as wild as the land, fleeing as I approached, before gathering on the crest of the hill to watch me. Above, a crow danced a welcome, its flight making the air's currents and eddies visible. It called with a voice soft and musical, the sound and rhythm reminding me of the island dialect. Did crows have accents, I wondered? 'Hello,' I said, first in my head, then out loud, my words carried with the wind.

Further into the hill, the ground became wetter and there were deep lines where peat had been cut. Some of the older banks were starting to sink in on themselves, while the sharp lines of others indicated recent work. Several small lochs dotted the hillside at irregular intervals, their water the dark brown of peat, their surfaces rolling and rippling. Other than a pair of whooper swans, startlingly white in the darkening day, I could see no other signs of life. Returning to the road and walking towards the northern tip of the island, I became suddenly aware of the presence of the sea all around, encircling me. The wind carried the sound of waves, bringing me closer to the swirling patterns of light and froth as they danced from the distant horizon. A network of fences separated this narrow strip of land into a patchwork of small asymmetrical fields. Some sheep and white geese grazed close to the shore, fleece and feathers moving with the wind.

As I explored over the next few days I met several more of our neighbours. The house we rented was one of five in a cluster. We lived in the house that had originally been owned by our landlord's parents, and the other four houses were owned by our landlord's aunts, uncles and nieces. As days passed, I learned that this pattern of living was common across the island. It was so different from the unrelated, self-contained households that I had known in cities. I worried that we would be seen as intruders, an unwelcome addition to the social life of the place, but from the moment we arrived we were greeted with warmth and kindness. Within days we had been invited to an eighteenth birthday party and to a neighbour's wedding. People would stop, chat, and tell us stories about the area and the folk who used to live in our house. These stories were filled with love, good humour and mischief. Many times we were told of our garden shed: 'Everybody calls that shed Chernobyl. Probably best you don't go inside.' We later learned that the shed had once caught fire, though its owner had insisted there had been nothing flammable inside. It later transpired that it had been 'full to bursting' with hay and engine oil. With each new story, or each old story repeated by a new voice, I felt more connected with the house and those who had called it home before. The various eccentricities of decor or wiring that we encountered now made the place feel more like home, and as I walked and saw other groups of houses huddled together in a wild landscape, I saw them as networks of connection and belonging.

During those first few weeks, the ever-changing quality of weather and light never ceased to amaze me. The sun remained low on the horizon, and on clear days it infused the air with golden light, so I felt suspended in perpetual sunset. The air was in constant motion, never falling below force 5 during my first few weeks on the island. Clouds, laden, low to the ground, carried with them fleeting rainbows as they sped past. Hailstones could suddenly appear from a clear sky, blown from distant clouds; whipped by the wind, they bounced and scattered before melting into the wet ground. The sea was continually changing shades from grey to blue and green, the motion of white-crested waves responding to signals from the sky. I felt energised and excited by this living world of weather, but I found the cold difficult to bear. I thought I had come prepared, with layers of clothing, thermals, waterproofs, hats and gloves, but when the wind blew from the north, carrying horizontal hailstones, I felt the cold slicing my face, leaving me with headaches that could last hours. I pulled my hat down low and wrapped my scarf over my nose and mouth, hastily unwrapping myself slightly if I saw other folk out walking.

Every conversation included a question about how I was finding the place. Did I like it here? The answer I wanted to give was that I thought it was magical. That walking among the wind, land and sea was telling me that the folk tales of mystery and hidden lives and worlds were true. That this place made me simultaneously calm and excited. How, although new to me, it felt deeply like somewhere I already knew. Unsure how this whimsical enthusiasm would be received in a community that is known for its pride in its hardworking, practical relationships with land, I tended to keep my answers more general. These suspicions were confirmed to me when some weeks later I responded to a question from an elderly gentleman by describing the beauty of the light. This was met with a long stare followed by a story about the time he'd taken an artist out on his boat. The artist had kept talking about the beautiful light but the man hadn't had time to look as he'd been working with his creels. The artist hadn't helped with the work, but had taken some of the lobster away with him! In time, I learned that these initial impressions I'd had about the relationships islanders have with place were not quite correct. Although practical concerns were central to crofting on the isle, their love for the land and for animals intermingled with rather more intangible feelings of home to form a rich social tapestry of belonging.

The storm

One morning, as I was getting ready to meet a research participant on the mainland, I nervously watched the waves crash against the rocks. The sea was a constant motion of rolling waves as far as my eye could see. I feared being left stranded if the island ferry was cancelled. I decided to be sensible and phone the ferry information line.

'Hello, I am just phoning to check if you think the weather might stop the Whalsay ferry running today?'

My enquiry was met with an initial silence followed by a slightly confused-sounding, 'What weather? Looks to be fine here daday.'

Waiting in line for the ferry, my apprehension grew as I heard the wind whistling through the masts of the fishing boats and felt my small car buffeted by the stronger gusts. This was the boat that I would need to take regularly to meet research participants. How would I manage this if I was scared of the boat? I felt like an imposter, unable to manage the basics of island life.

As the boat moved out of the harbour, my whole body was tense. I stepped out of the car and walked towards the porthole, hoping that seeing land would ease my worries slightly. I stood braced, waiting for the motion of the waves, but the journey was remarkably smooth.

After a lovely afternoon chatting about ponies over cups of tea and braving the wind to go out to the fields to meet them, I drove back to the ferry. The wind seemed stronger, but again the boat chugged along smoothly. When I got back to Vevoe, Robbie was working in his shed and I said how surprised I'd been that the boat was OK in such a gale. He said that the ferry could take a fair gale from that direction but that the storm was just beginning and was forecast to get considerably worse over the next few days.

Overnight the wind worked itself up to storm force. Rain battered the windows and I heard the roar from the sea as the force of the waves moved the stones on the beach. The wind surrounded the house, rising from a low hum to a piercing howl, forcing its way in through door and window frames, breaking the boundaries between inside and out. My phone bleeped, an automated message from the ferry to say the Whalsay service was suspended due to adverse weather. I put torches beside the bed and placed candles in holders in strategic locations across the house, anticipating a power cut. I was intensely aware of being cut off, from Shetland, and from the rest of the UK. I was now stranded on this tiny island while days of storms raged. I lay in bed as the house shook with the larger gusts.

I woke with the first rays of sunshine. The storm had not lessened – if anything the wind felt stronger. I stepped outside; instantly I felt the wind catch me. Almost losing my footing, I trotted sideways a few steps before correcting my course and walking un-steadily to the rocks above the shore. The sea was a living mass of energy, steel-grey and froth-frenzied. Waves reared high, revealing a turquoise underbelly, before crashing onto the rocks. Salt spray, whipped from the wave crests, filled the air with a salt-laden glaze. Unable to safely keep my footing, I sat on the sodden ground.

The world felt like it was vibrating in response to the deep, thundering roar of the waves, while the wind blew, buffeted and cajoled. In the moments between waves I saw dark shapes move underwater. Seals. Selkies. In Shetland folklore, these beings who inhabit worlds of land and sea may take on human form. I watched as they flitted between the waves, hunting, visible for a moment then gone. In time, I would learn to know this as the wind that brought gannets to our bay. Above the waves they flew, flashing brilliant white, as they dived into the deep, emerging moments later to rejoin the circling birds in the sky. As the wind blew from me to them, I felt a lingering sense of connection to these other beings, to their lives of sea and sky. My body and mind felt alert, enlivened by this frenzied tempest, taking joy from being still while simultaneously part of this world of motion.

2

LEANDRA

I WOKE TO A WORLD transformed. An uncanny silence after weeks of battering winds revealed a snow-covered landscape. Flakes drifted slowly down, their gentle descent through motionless air a stark contrast to the horizontal hailstones that had stung my face just the day before. With their blanket of snow, the surrounding hills appeared smaller and closer, their shape softened. Sheep with icicled fleece grazed by the roadside. I drove slowly over the uneven track that led to the small croft where Bjørn was already outside, wearing a bright knitted jumper and woollen hat, carrying a feed bucket. He greeted me enthusiastic-ally, as his German shepherd Amina chased the snowballs he threw. 'Come with me, it is time to feed the ponies,' he said, setting off across the yard.

As a young boy growing up in Norway, Bjørn had fallen in love with horses. His first horse had been a

Shetland pony, and over the years, his passion for the breed had grown. Admitting, with a grin, that he never did things by halves, Bjørn said, 'So I had to move to Shetland – for the ponies.' After years of planning, visiting and dreaming, he and his partner had settled in Shetland where they had a pony stud with around eighty Shetland ponies. 'Look around.' He gestured. 'This is the home of the Shetland pony. It is where they belong and they love it here.'

As we stepped into the closest field, tiny ponies soon approached. Golden palomino, rich chestnut, dark brown and many colours in between shone against the white of the ground. Their breath visible in the cold, they whickered to each other and nuzzled at Bjørn's hands. A brown-and-white pony came quietly over to me and sniffed at my pockets before starting to chew a section of my hair. I felt a sudden rush of joy as I felt the warmth of its body and the sweet scent of hay surrounding me.

'These are the peerie foals, they get extra feed as it is their first winter,' he said, as he placed food into troughs. The starlings who had been perched ready on the fence began to come closer, eating any food the ponies dropped. A loud *baa*-ing echoed through the still landscape as a small flock of sheep galloped to join us. Leading them was a large moorit ram with impressive horns and several multi-coloured Shetland sheep. 'You will have to wait,' Bjorn told the noisy crowd. 'Harbro will deliver hard feed tomorrow, and then you will get some.' The sheep ignored his words and continued to follow us as we walked through the fields, dashing up to us and *baa*-ing insistently each time we stopped.

Once the ponies close to the croft had been fed it was time to find the hill herd. Although he was pleased that the frost had brought an end to the winter's squelchy mud, Bjørn was concerned that this sudden extreme cold would make fresh, unfrozen water difficult to find. Armed with a length of metal pipe, Bjørn and I set off across the hill. As we walked, he pointed out walls, ridges and hollows that are favourite places for ponies to shelter from bad weather. I listened, amazed at his knowledge and at how differently he saw the land. For me it had appeared as an empty expanse but for Bjørn it was a home to his horses, filled with stories and significant places.

He criss-crossed the field, moving directly towards all the places where he knew there was usually water. Every time he found it frozen. He would break through the ice with the metal pole only to find more layers of thicker ice underneath. As he checked the few remaining places for water, he appeared worried. 'This has never happened before,' he said. 'We need to get water to the horses.'

In the distance, some horses were standing, their shapes dark against the snowy landscape. One horse, an older mare called Leandra, started to move towards us. 'She is thirsty, she will need our help,' Bjørn said as she approached.

Before she reached us, Leandra turned, and walked towards the hill, where she stopped and seemed to be drinking, even though there appeared to be no sign of water. Once we were beside her, we could see a small puddle. On closer inspection, we realised that this puddle was being fed by a stream just below the ground that remained unfrozen. Bjørn started to dig at the area, making the hole bigger to make it easier for the other ponies to drink from. I was amazed: not only had Leandra known how to find water, but she had effectively shared that knowledge with Bjorn and the other ponies in the herd.

As we worked Bjørn told me: 'Here the ponies are in the right environment. It is the same as if you wanted to make wine, for example – you wouldn't live in Norway, or here. I am a great believer that if you are going to breed good ponies you need to breed them in the right environment. This is where they come from, this is where they should live, and do you know Darwin's discovery about animals across the Galapagos Islands? How the breeds change from island to island, even across a very short distance. That is very interesting, and it is the same with horses.'

He described how the Shetland pony became the way it is today because of centuries living within Shetland's landscapes, walking long distances to find food and learning to shelter from the elements. Like many other pony breeders I would meet, Bjørn emphasised the importance of giving ponies a chance to live in the types of environment that is natural for them. It is by living in this type of place, with freedom to think and learn, that they gain the type of intelligence Leandra had displayed. She was able to find water where her human owner could not. With this knowledge she could lead the herd to water, keeping them safe in this frozen landscape. This ability to adapt to changing and challenging environmental conditions is one of the most valued characteristics in Shetland ponies.

Even in Shetland it can be difficult to keep ponies naturally, as there are no longer the huge areas of shared hill grazing that were once common. Bjørn was trying to recreate the types of landscape that Shetland ponies would have traditionally lived in by making inventive use of his land. Throughout winter, he continually monitored the conditions of the fields and the health of the ponies to ensure he did not give too little or too much feed. Where possible, he kept his ponies in large areas of hill park where they could move around to find food and shelter for themselves. Even if they did not spend all their lives in fields like this, having some experience of this natural life would help keep alive their knowledge and natural instincts.

As we returned to the road, a lone sheep walked towards us and then stood still, her yellow eyes fixed on us. Bjørn sighed and threw some hay to her. She immediately started to eat, not taking her eyes off us. Bjørn told me how sad he is for this sheep. 'There were two sheep,' he said, 'always together, but the other one died and this one is now always alone. I always give her some hay to make her a little happier.' We watched as this lonely sheep, her head and back covered in ice and snow, finished her hay and walked slowly back to the hill. Over the following months, I would learn that this type of love and attention towards Shetland's native breeds is an important part of how people share a landscape with these wise, adaptable breeds.

The flock next door

Stepping outside one morning, after the snow had melted, I saw a man standing by the gate of the sheep field. Dressed entirely in dark blue waterproofs, the figure was uttering a single repeating sound: 'Kid! Kid! Kid! Kid!' The sheep, which had until then seemed so wild to me, galloped towards the gate. In their excitement, some leaped into the air, bouncing down the hill. Catching sight of me, the man smiled and said, 'They're just like peerie lambs sometimes.' He threw some sheep nuts over the fence and most of the sheep gathered around, eating. 'Some are more tame than others,' he added, throwing some nuts to the sheep that had stayed further back, watching me somewhat warily. He introduced himself as Lowrie. In his seventies, he'd grown up on the isle, and the area by our house was part of his family croft.

Watching the sheep, Lowrie noted that they didn't really need much feeding, even at this time of year, since they could find plenty on the hill and could go down onto the beach to get seaweed. Looking towards the horizon, where the sun was partially obscured by clouds, he said the light was starting to return. This would soon bring the new growth of seaweed, the food the sheep liked best, and the flock would gather by the ebb. They always knew when it was time. 'Watching sheep can teach you a lot,' he said, 'and sheep are far cleverer than most people think.' Each one was an individual, he said, and as you spent time with them you got to know what they were like. Laughing, he told me a story about a crofter who had brought his three sheep inside the crofthouse one winter. The first morning, he was puzzled to find the sheep in a brightly lit room when he was sure he had turned the light off the night before. The next morning the same thing happened. On the third night, after he turned off the light and closed the door, he waited. Sure enough, he saw the light go on. The sheep had learned to pull the cord that switched the light on and off. Another flock he knew kept escaping to a field they were not supposed to be in. Over and over they were moved to different places but the sheep always found their way back. Frustrated, the crofter eventually decided to take the sheep to their new field by boat so that they could not find their way back. They were back in the forbidden field before the crofter and boat got home. Lowrie said that the intelligence and hardiness of Shetland breeds is remarkable, and that life would have been impossible in the past without them.

He described how in the past all of the crofts would have had a cow that would be in the fields closest to the croft, kept in at night and fed extra scraps from the kitchen. He said his aunt, who'd had this croft before him, had had a cow who wouldn't allow anyone to milk her unless she was brushed at the same time. He said he found it quite frustrating as a child, having to spend hours brushing this stubborn cow, but he now knew just how important it was to learn to understand and respect individual animals when you were working with them. As he turned to get onto his quad bike home, he told me that if I wanted to get to know his sheep I was welcome to throw them some sheep nuts so that they would come to me. Neither of us knew that I would not only grow to love these sheep, but that I would soon introduce a little orphan lamb into their midst.

Island life

Steve and I had been careful to never lock the front door again, but we'd assumed that visitors would still knock and wait for you to answer. We quickly learned this wasn't the case. Neighbours just opened the door, walked several steps into the hall calling, 'Onybody hame?' or 'Aye-aye?' to alert us to their presence. Visiting is such a part of island culture that the assumption is that at any point in the day you are happy for somebody to come into your home. This was completely alien to me and made me feel rather uncomfortable at first. As somebody who is often in a state of disorganised chaos, when I am expecting visitors I will usually do a manic burst of tidying to give a veneer of order. But that wasn't an option here: people could pop in *at any time*. One morning, I stepped out of the bathroom after a shower wearing only a small towel at the same moment that somebody walked through the door. This led to me ensuring I was always fully dressed before venturing anywhere in the house.

After the initial shock of neighbours walking into our house, we started to enjoy the familiarity of such encounters. Often it was Robbie or Ina, coming to see how we were getting on, and telling us stories and useful information. Robbie told me that when, generations ago, his family had first moved to Vevoe, they could see the fires over on Fetlar that were part of the Highland Clearances. He explained that the dips we saw across the coastline were places where kelp had been burned and the ash used for glass or soap, and he advised us on some of the best places to look for otters. Ina told us stories about the places she'd played as a child, and spoke about the social and economic changes that had taken place on the isle in her lifetime. Lowrie told me stories of sheep, and detailed all the bird species that visited the island and when I could expect to see them. These conversations became a regular part of my days, expanding my knowledge of the landscape around me, affecting my experiences and making walking a much more sociable activity.

I noticed that every house, including ours, had a pair of binoculars. At first I'd assumed they were for birdwatching, but over time I realised they had a more social function. As I visited folk I noticed they would regularly use their binoculars to observe boats on the water, to see who was visiting another house, or to check on an animal they could see in the distance.

I thought back to my first few days on the island: whenever I met new people they would often say, 'I've seen you out walking,' and it dawned on me that they might have seen me a little closer than I had initially thought. I began to see houses as sentient, part of a watchful network that made the empty landscape I walked along feel more inhabited.

Connections between houses was more than simply keeping note of the day's activity: vast histories of people and places were woven into island life. Some houses were still known by the names of people who had lived there before such as 'Beenie's house' along the road from us, and stories always mentioned specifically where events took place as well as details about who was present. People were also connected to places through their names. Names like Robbie or John were very common on the island, so our neighbour Robbie was known as Robbie o' Vevoe, and Willie who had lived in our house before us was Willie o' Vevoe. This name often did not change if you left, so if Robbie were to move to Huxter, he would be 'Robbie o' Vevoe dat bydes in Huxter'.

These names, stories and places felt like they had a life of their own, building the social fabric of the islands. When Shetland people meet, they will often catch up on local news, discussing who has recently married, moved house or changed job. From these seemingly simple beginnings, conversations will often branch out to include friends or extended family of those discussed, a brief update on the social history of an area. If people meet who don't know one another, they will often start asking about people they might know: 'Ah, du bydes in Burra, dus du ken auld Gordon o' Freefield?' And so on until they have traced a path to a common connection, in a practice known as 'reddin up kin'. It was the details of these conversations that really amazed me, how distant and extended families were remembered, drawn into everyday life, creating and maintaining connections and belonging.

I loved the sociality of island life, but the more I understood about the extent of people's layers of belonging and connectedness the more it seemed to be something I could never truly be a part of. I struggled to remember people's names and where they lived, details that seemed essential to everyday life on the island. Also, spending so much time off island for fieldwork meant I didn't have as much time to participate in local events as I would have liked. I knew people were watching us, trying to figure out who we were and what sort of residents we would be. I wanted to fit in, for people to like us, but I was also anxious, worried about getting things wrong.

Stories of island domestication

Since childhood I've had favourite breeds of horse, longing to one day have my own Connemara or Arab, without ever giving much thought to the concept of breed or the meanings I attached to animals based on their breed identity. Before I moved to Shetland, I conducted extensive book-based research on the role of breed in human–animal relationships, and was surprised to learn that distinguishing between animals based on breed was a relatively new practice and one closely associated with ideas of domination and class politics. The idea of breed took hold in Britain during the eighteenth and nineteenth centuries. Some of this breed creation was directed towards identifiable goals (breeding faster racehorses or increasing the milk yield of cattle, for example), but aesthetics was also an important part of the story. Beauty of form was rewarded at shows, and particularly good examples of a breed could become minor celebrities, touring the countryside attracting large crowds and becoming household names. Most of these early experiments in breeding were conducted by wealthy landowners who were credited as designers, creating these breeds through their hard work and imagination. The animals themselves were seen as passive in the process, like clay to be moulded. In his article

'Corpulent Cattle and Milk Machines: Nature, Art and the Ideal Type', Michael Quinn describes how this narrative of power over nature was used to further justify the position of the aristocracy, who claimed it as evidence of their right to control the lives of the humans and animals on their land.

As I travelled around Shetland, I quickly learned that local stories of breed were very different. I was told that to understand Shetland breeds I needed to know the history of crofting, how people and animals had learned to live together. At 60 degrees north, where the island's small areas of fertile ground are surrounded by acres of rough heather hill, and gale-force winds scour the land, making a living from agriculture is a challenge. Each croft would only have a small patch of cultivatable land and shared access to wild expanses of hill. The lairds, who owned the land crofters rented, operated an exploitative system of debt bondage that forced the crofting population to give up almost everything they produced in exchange for a few overpriced items. With little access to cash, and often with large debts to their landlords, crofters needed to use their land in a way that allowed them to produce almost everything they needed to survive.

This geography combined with the difficult travel conditions to and from the islands contributed to the development of several distinct breeds of domestic animals. Small, hardy and adaptable, these animals could live in places that most domestic breeds could not. Sheep and ponies thrived in the rough hill and, because they required little attention, were cheap to keep. Sheep's wool was spun, dyed and turned into the famous Shetland knitwear, which was a vital source of income. Shetland ponies were used on the croft for draught purposes, carrying people and goods across the countryside, but the role they are most celebrated for was bringing home the peat. During the summer, crofters worked in the hill, cutting peat and stacking it on top of the banks to dry. Often when I visited pony breeders they would show me old photographs of lines of Shetland ponies with heavy baskets attached to their sides, bringing home the peat that would have been a croft's only source of heat that winter. An iconic story of heat, light, survival and hope. Were it not for the hardy Shetland breed's ability to thrive within such landscapes while providing essential household resources, life in Shetland would have been impossible. In direct contrast to breeds invented by the rich to exert control, these Shetland breeds are not thought of as something manufactured by ingenious humans, but as active participants in positive lives and landscapes. Humans and animals lived and adapted together, finding ways to belong and thrive in Shetland's wild landscapes. In fact, by providing resources for little cost, these intelligent companions on the croft actually enabled Shetlanders to resist some of the landowner's tyranny.

During my first months in Shetland, I was amazed how similar these stories were, all focusing on the difficulty of crofting life, and the resourcefulness of people and animals who survived it. Across the islands, museums and history groups curated photos and archive materials, creating displays and online resources. This was not aimed towards visitors, although everyone was welcomed to these spaces; it was Shetland people telling and retelling their history. Unwillingly, I found myself remembering some academic articles I had read prior to fieldwork that claimed Shetlanders' attention towards aspects of their own history was a fetishised or false nostalgia. Yet even with the similarity, and the sometimes slightly institutionalised nature of these histories, this did not feel true. It was only after I spent a day with Gary, as he recounted his life with animals, that I began to have a better understanding of the nature of history as part of contemporary social life.

While Gary made me a cup of tea, I glanced around his living room. The walls, dressers and tables were filled with pictures, photographs and ornaments, neatly arranged without a speck of dust on them. Many of the ornaments featured rural scenes with ponies and workhorses. I have never liked these types of decoration. They always seemed twee and false, belonging to a world of chocolate-box images, celebrating and representing an imagined rural ideal.

As we sat with our tea, Gary talked about growing up in Shetland, of crofters, peat banks, and long summer days spent with the hill ponies. His stories were alive with detail: memories of watching horses as they made their way across the hill; of crouching low to the ground, cautiously approaching mares with foals, gradually getting closer, until finally they allowed him to touch them. He described the feel of the rope in his hands as he struggled to hold on, while foals unfamiliar with the halter twisted, pulled and tried to bolt. He and his friend had spent hours outside with the horses, enjoying spending time with them, rarely with any adult instruction or interference.

He walked over to a shelf and picked up a small model, of a foal prancing. 'Every year my favourite mare had a foal and they were always like this one,' he said, handing me the model. 'Full of mischief and wild as the heather. Fine foals though. Always got a good price.'

When he was older, Gary had moved away from Shetland and had spent many years working in farms in Scotland. He stood up and took another model horse down from the shelf. He ran his hands over the ornament, highlighting certain features as he described the farm horses and how they differed from the ponies from his youth. Later, when describing a pair of horses he used for ploughing, he pointed to another model. He said they look so exactly like the horses he knew that it was remarkable, like having a photograph of them. He smiled as he spoke about his horses, telling me about their personalities and the work they did. Bringing the statue closer, he pointed out details on the plough and how the harnesses fitted to the horses, and explained in detail about days spent on the farm.

As I drove home my thoughts returned to the horse ornaments. Although on the surface they had appeared to me as generic images of a rural ideal, that afternoon they had come alive through Gary's stories. Their presence in his living room was an ongoing reminder of relationships with horses he knew and loved. I realised that although there was an element of nostalgia in historic rememberings, this did not mean those stories were not also important and true.

Stories can create a sense of home, can tell us about who we are and who we want to be. By telling them we can make and remake the worlds we live in. The stories of crofting history reveal some of the things people value most about the distinct Shetland way of life. Although hardship and exploitation were features of these narratives, it was the independence and resilience of the crofting folk that stories really focused on. How communities worked together, helping one another in times of hardship and celebrating together in times of joy.

Shetland breeds, due to their intelligence, adaptability and companionship, became valued members of crofting households. Had their animals required expensive feed, indoor shelter, or intensive amounts of human attention, crofting life would have been impossible. As people work with native breeds today, remembering the animals in Shetland past shapes these relationships, as people continue to value and promote the breeds' historic qualities. And so the past isn't something separate and distant from contemporary social life, but rather, I learned, it was a living, adaptive and practical part of ensuring island futures in a rapidly changing world.

At home within changing landscapes

One of the first conversations I had with June, who had spent her life with ponies, helped me understand the deep connections between people, animals and landscapes today. She said: 'For us, ponies are a way of life – they are my partners, not my pets. I have learned so much over the years from watching ponies being ponies, and they never fail to come up with something new to amaze me. Many things have no explanation but I would always put my trust in a Shetland pony.

The ponies with access to the seashore always come down from the hills to eat seaweed at the ebb tide. How do they know when low tide is when the time changes every day? They always know the day before a gale comes and from what direction it is coming – how? They come down off the hill at the same time each day in winter to be fed – how do they know the time when the length of daylight changes each day? There's a lot us humans can learn from animals if we just take the time to watch. In Shetland so much of our lives depends on the land and weather around us. We Shetlanders notice the small things: when the oyster-catchers and bonxies come back, we notice the seasons, and we know the times for things. People have lost so much knowledge and instinct about life and the world. Maybe by watching we can get some of it back. Watch and they can point us in the right direction. But if we lose it, and take it from them, we might not get it back.'

Talk of change and preserving skills for the future were always part of conversations about crofting life. Changes to agriculture and the wider economy in Shetland mean today crofting often brings in little income compared to other work, and the majority of crofters and pony breeders have at least one other type of employment. Despite the lack of financial incentives to take part in agricultural work, with many describing the challenging economic realities of continuing these traditional activities, crofting remains a passion for many people as family crofts continue to be passed down to the next generation.

It wasn't long after I'd moved to Shetland that I first visited Burland Croft on Trondra, perhaps the best-known place for Shetland breeds. It was a gorgeous, bright morning and the surfaces of the lochs were smooth, reflecting the hills and sky. With a shock I realised that this was the first time I had seen this phenomenon in Shetland. I had grown accustomed to lochs with ripples and sometimes surprisingly large waves as they moved with the wind, but today the wind had dropped. 'Light air force 1,' confirmed the local radio weather report, which gives regular updates on where the wind falls on the Beaufort scale.

As I drove over the small bridge that connects the island of Trondra to the mainland, a flock of Shetland geese helped me identify the correct road to take to the croft, their grey and white feathers bright in the sun. Mary and Tommy met me at the door and invited me into their kitchen. As I admired a painting of a Shetland cow on the wall, Mary told me that when they started the croft they'd wanted to buy Shetland native breeds but were shocked to discover how few of these animals remained. The market demand for large carcass size had resulted in many crofters cross-breeding the naturally small Shetland cow with larger cattle breeds. Within just a few generations, the number of native cattle had reduced dramatically. Determined to prevent the breed's extinction, Mary and Tommy began searching for the remaining cattle across the islands. Over the following years, numbers of native cattle slowly began to rise, as more crofts began to keep this ancient breed once more. They'd developed their poultry flock by looking out for birds of the types that most resembled the old Shetland breeds, and by speaking to crofters to learn about the types of birds they remembered. Over time, they had created breeding flocks of all three types of Shetland poultry breed. The ducks especially are becoming a familiar sight around Shetland, as many crofters choose to have some native ducks in addition to their other animals.

Whenever I visited Mary and Tommy I was welcomed with a cup of tea, homemade cakes and stories. Throughout these stories, the interconnected lives of people and animals were always present. Mary and Tommy believed that crofts should have a responsibility that stretched beyond their individual croft to include plants and animals in the surrounding landscape. Shetland breeds were described as perfectly adapted, both physically and mentally, to Shetland landscapes and traditional crofting practices. The animals are happy with this life, they thrive given the space and independence to live relatively naturally, and crofters can produce healthy animals with less time or financial commitment than larger breeds require. In this way, animals, people and place can continue to live, thrive and belong together.

The large windows offered views across the croft: on one side, the rough hill ground, on the other, lush green grass that stretched to a pebbly beach where two boats bobbed in the bay. As we sat with tea or walked about the land, Mary and Tommy would comment on the movements of birds and animals. They talked about when the sheep went to the shore to eat seaweed, the behaviour of the crows in relation to crofting activities, and where the ducks were currently trying to build nests. They told stories of the Shetland cattle they had, one who loved people and would gallop to the fence whenever a bus arrived, another that refused to be milked by humans but tried to give milk to any cow, or even sheep, that was in her field. Each cow had its own unique personality. I learned about their hardy sheep living out on an island, which they only saw a few times a year for essential care. They spoke, too, of their tame lambs, which the visitors loved to meet and feed with a bottle.

From where we sat we had a clear view down to the beach, and once watched as a flock of sheep walked in a line, heading towards the shore. 'They're a bit late today,' Tommy said to Mary, who nodded her agreement. Tommy turned to me and said, 'You can learn a lot by watching: these Shetland sheep are very clever. Have you heard of hefted sheep?'

I said that I had: the area I grew up in had flocks of sheep who were deeply connected to the particular area of hill where they were born.

'Well, it's like these sheep are hefted to Shetland – they know the hill, and the weather.' He went on to describe how crofters and sheep learn this landscape in relation to one another, and how these rhythms of landscape and crofting life are passed down through generations, human and animal.

Mary said it was the same with the ducks. 'They belong here. The ducks and the place just fit together,' she said, describing her joy at seeing their numbers increase across the islands.

Mary and Tommy, like many other crofters and pony breeders that I met, feared that declining numbers of native breeds worldwide would result in a harmful monoculture of domestic animals. Losing breeds that have developed to suit various regional niches would put farming in geographically peripheral areas such as Shetland particularly at risk. Larger breeds require additional shelter and imported feed, costing more to keep and leaving island crofters at the mercy of the changing feed and transport costs. Without the native breeds that have the ability to thrive in Shetland, crofting could become unaffordable. While people and animals continue to learn in relation to each other and the environment, they actively cultivate the possibility of happy, sustainable and independent life in the islands. As new generations work on crofts and pony studs, and wider social relationships with land and animals change, so practices continue to adapt. For a time it seemed that the only economically viable method of farming was the system that prioritised high volume and cheap cost. However, recent years have seen a sustained shift in consumer preferences towards artisan meat and dairy products. Many who work with Shetland native breeds emphasise the high quality of their produce. The meat from livestock raised on the hill, eating heather, wildflowers and seaweed, has a depth of flavour missing from most commercially produced livestock. In addition to superior taste, scientific research suggests that that these native-breed products may also offer additional health benefits compared to those from intensively reared livestock. Seeing new possibilities for these ancient breeds, there is an increased focus on promoting high-quality healthy and environmentally friendly food from Shetland.

Crofting life in Shetland depends on a particular type of engaged attention. Anna Lowenhaupt Tsing, in her book *The Mushroom at the End of the World*, writes about the complex networks of relationships between mushroom pickers and the forests where they work. Successful mushroom picking requires extensive knowledge of history and ecology. She describes how these pickers cultivate an art of noticing, a form of attention that allows them to understand the multiple lives within the forest. Crofters and pony breeders, through their acts, and arts, of noticing, cultivate relationships with their animals based on care and attention. By sharing their lives with animals they are connecting, and reconnecting, to ways of life that must not be forgotten. Lessons from history combine with knowledge that emerges through everyday encounters with animals. People and animals learn with and from each other, as they adjust the rhythms of their life in relation to each other, and in response to wider economic and climatic patterns. An openness and an adaptability is central to this: being and belonging flows from ongoing, changing relationships. In an island community, past survival and future sustainability depend on the community taking care of one another, and this community extends to the lives of animals and landscapes. Through their continued love and attention, crofters and pony breeders continue to learn, and through teaching these ways they give the gift of 'Shetland as home' to future generations.

Crofting landscapes

On a stormy January day, I stopped by Tesco before catching the ferry home. I knew the boat connecting Shetland to the UK had been cancelled because of the weather, so I expected some shortages, but as I walked through the shop I saw row after row of empty shelves. There were no vegetables, chilled products or bread; even the cans and frozen goods were severely depleted. The winter before I'd moved to Shetland the storms had been so severe and had lasted for so long that food was delivered to the islands by military aircraft. When we'd arrived in Whalsay, neighbours had told us about the lack of food in shops during periods of bad weather, often illustrating the point with anecdotes about pan-icked incomers fighting over the last loaf of bread. I'd got a little over enthusiastic in my desire not to get caught out and become one of *those* incomers. I'd bought lots of cans and frozen goods, but the more I'd thought about it the longer the list got. What if we had a headache or a cold? Would shops run out of painkill-ers? How many toilet rolls were in Shetland at any given time, and how quickly might these run out? So as I walked through the empty shop, I felt a sense of relief, knowing I had plenty of food and supplies.

When I got home, I went for a walk in the hill,

enjoying the feeling of being surrounded by wind and waves. I thought about Tesco's empty shelves, something that would never happen in the mainland UK, but was an expected part of life here. Suddenly the mainland felt very far away, and I began to better understand Shetlanders' desire to preserve a degree of independence in their daily lives. Those who had a croft or whose family had land and could produce their own food had plenty for times of shortage, and had the ability to produce more. But the continuing value of traditional skills was about more than just having enough to cover the few days in winter when Tesco ran out, it was about having the means to provide for themselves, whatever future changes might occur.

Shetland's difficult historic relationships with those in power in the south mean there is little trust that Britain would prioritise island interests.

When the oil industry declines, and Shetland is of less strategic importance, then many jobs and opportunities will vanish.

Shetlanders are very aware that they will need to adapt to these economic shifts, and continuing crofting traditions and working to preserve local breeds are central to many islanders' hopes of remaining culturally and economically independent.

Although I saw no people as I walked in the gale, all around me was tradition and invention, the continuation of an ancient way of life into the future. A land inhabited by hopes and stories. Across the hill were small circular walls called planticrubs. In these tiny walled gardens people would have planted kale seed, so they'd be protected from every wind direction. This hardy Shetland kale fed both humans and animals throughout the year. Here the walls still stood, stone memories in the landscape, while in the houses around me, many people had packets of kale seeds, ready to plant when the season changed.

For the first time I really noticed the evidence of reuse and recycling. For so long, replacement items would have been hard to get so people had had to adapt. Although Whalsay is a relatively wealthy island, and online deliveries usually arrive within days, people will often reuse and mend rather than replace items. As I stood at the top of the hill I saw old boiler suits in their new roles as scarecrows, battered buckets repaired with twine, vintage bathtubs filled with water for livestock, and sheds roofed by boats that were no longer seaworthy but were still waterproof. I watched Lowrie's sheep make their way to the beach, free to roam yet provided with a few extra sheep nuts by a crofter who loved them.

As I walked down the hill I noticed I was moving my body in relation to the wind, turning slightly to lean in to the gale and shortening my steps, adopting a crab-like gait. As I moved with the air around me, I finally understood the truth of the jokes that when the wind stops blowing, Shetlanders all fall over. A force 8 gale is known as 'a guid drying day', and folk often hang out laundry on wild days – it just takes a little practice. My first attempt to hang out laundry was somewhat unsuccessful. Regardless of how carefully I tried to position myself, I was repeatedly slapped in the face by wet clothing. Soon after, a neighbour came to the door, to return my TOO COOL FOR YULE pyjamas that had blown into their garden. Hopes that my washing-line woes had gone unnoticed receded further as they recommended I stand side-on to the gale, and that I may want to buy some 'storm pegs'.

One day, as I moved around the line, dodging the sheets that flapped in the wind, I had the feeling I was being watched. Sure enough, a line of woolly faces had appeared on the crest of the hill. Ever since Lowrie had said I could feed them, whenever I saw the sheep I had thrown some nuts over the fence for them. Each time they turned to flee, only coming back to eat once I had gone. I went to get the feed bucket, rattling it at the gate while they stood and watched. One sheep in particular, with a charcoal-grey fleece and a black face, seemed to be paying attention. As I rattled the bucket again, she bounded at full speed, bouncing several times as she made her descent towards the gate. As if woken from a trance, the other sheep followed and began to eat the nuts. Overenthusiastically, I threw another scoop towards them, the sudden motion causing the flock to dart backwards, before creeping forward once again. The grey sheep was closest to the gate and beside her stood a large moorit wether, the asymmetrical white line down his face and tendency to stare directly at you giving him a distinctly eccentric appearance.

A few days later, while walking on the hill, I heard a noise behind me. Turning, I saw the whole flock standing looking at me. As I began to walk I heard it again. The sound of many hoofs trotting through heather. Again, as soon as I turned to look at them they froze. I decided to change my route, now heading towards home and the bucket of sheep nuts. They followed, getting closer and closer as I neared the gate. I rushed to get their food, and as I threw it to them, only one sheep ran away: a scrawny brown yowe with a white forehead who from that moment became known as Scaredy Sheep. I was delighted at my newfound friends, writing in my fieldnotes that they'd followed me home, before reflecting that as I had changed direction in response to their desire for food, had they, in fact, actually led me?

As January became February then March, the quality of the light began to change as the sun rose higher in the sky. Daylight stretched towards the evenings and an intense clarity replaced the sense of eternal twilight. The world appeared as if awoken, the contours of hills defined, sea and sky bright and the horizon sharp. The starlings and sparrows chattered with renewed vigour, and Lowrie confirmed that they had started investigating nest sites. With this new light came the sound of the oystercatcher, known in Shetland as shalder. Lowrie and Robbie for weeks had been telling me to listen out for the shrill piping cry that means spring is on its way. Suddenly they were everywhere, orange bills coated in earth as they dug in fields and by roadsides. Despite Robbie confirming that the pair on the beach nested there every year, each time the sheep passed, the birds rose in alarm, wings beating, their warnings carried with the wind. Fulmar had been present throughout the winter but now their numbers increased. Pairs glided past, wings outstretched, with each pass coming a little closer, silent, eyes fixed on me. Soon, I hoped, they'd find nooks and crevices along the rugged coastline to raise their young. In sheltered spots, behind walls or in gardens, the first crocuses emerged, tiny brave splashes of colour, a vibrant presence in a landscape scoured by a winter of salt-laden storms. A new sound emerged from the hill, lilting notes carried on the wind: the song of the skylark, the sound that islanders associate with the true end of winter. I listened as this tiny bird heralded the start of my first Shetland spring.

3

YODA

TWO PAIRS OF EYES LOOKED at me from across the
table, waiting for my response. A third pair joined
them as the four-day-old lamb cradled in my arms
stopped drinking from his bottle and looked up at me.
We looked at each other for a moment and he let out
a tiny, squeaky, gurgling, '*Baaaa.*'

'He's your lambie now.' Suddenly the inevitability
of the situation hit me: I was leaving with this lamb. I'd
been excited when one of my research participants
had said another pony breeder would be coming by
with a caddy (bottle-fed) lamb. And now here I was,
the owner of a tiny sheep. For every question or objec-
tion I had, there was an answer ready: 'Here is some
powdered milk and a bottle, you can get more from
the vet's on your way home.' 'He will be no bother,
just give him his bottle four times a day.' 'Your husband
will *love* him. No, no – don't call him to check.'

I drove home in a state of panic. Where would he live? How did you look after a lamb? And what would Steve say when I came home with a sheep?! I had really wanted the lamb, but reality was beginning to sink in: I now owned an animal that I had little idea how to take care of. I tried to concentrate on driving, trying to forget he was there, telling myself to worry about it later. This was easier said than done when at every corner there was a soft thump as he lost his balance, followed by a scuffle as he stood up again.

Waiting at the ferry terminal I took a picture of the lamb and sent it to Steve with the message: *I got you a present.* Arriving home, however, it was clear from his initial enthusiasm that the signal had not been strong enough to send the photo, and he had only received part of the message. As he opened the back door of the car, the lamb stood on wobbly legs and emitted a loud, insistent bleat.

'Where is that going to go?' Steve asked. 'And how long is it here for?' I suddenly became aware of how badly the lamb smelled. He was absolutely coated in dried mud and poo, and the journey in a hot car seemed to have ripened him. His owner had said that he was one of a pair of twins, and that the mother had accepted only one – the weaker-looking twin, oddly – and had rejected him. She'd watched, hoping the mother would come to her senses, but the little lamb had wandered from sheep to sheep trying to get some milk. The other yowes had chased him while his mother took no notice. 'He is a fighter and a survivor,' she had said.

There was no way he could sleep outside, alone, it would be far too cold, and so we made him a little home in the garage. This would be temporary, I assured Steve. The lamb would learn to live with Lowrie's flock – I would not let him become a pet and would spend the summer teaching him to be a sheep.

We opened the garden gate and in he bounced, sniffing at flowers and seemingly unfazed by his new surroundings. Within a few minutes of the lamb exiting the car, one of the children next door appeared. As the boy ran through the garden the lamb followed, bouncing high in the air, tiny hoofs kicking to the side.

'What are you goin tae call him?' he asked. I looked at the lamb, who stood still and serene, his ears comically large, and I realised the date. May the 4th. Star Wars Day.

'Yoda,' I replied with a smile. After a few more minutes playing with Yoda, the little boy said he had better go home. Folk on the ferry had seen I had an animal in the car and had called our neighbours to update them on this development. They had been worried I had got a dog, and he needed to go and tell them that it was just a sheep.

With a basin filled with warm water and several old cloths and towels on standby, it was time to bath Yoda. He was far too small and at risk of the cold to place him in the water so Steve held him still while I combed and wiped at his fleece, trying to remove the larger chunks of dirt. There was a constant clattering of hoofs as he protested this treatment and tried to wiggle free. I wrapped him in a blanket and took him into the house to warm up. His dark blue-black eyes began to close as I slowly rubbed him with the towel, and before long he was asleep on my knee, snoring slightly. I was instantly and completely in love with this little orphan lamb.

Most of my earliest childhood memories involve the animals that I shared my life and home with. For a time we rented a house that came with a goat, and we soon borrowed a donkey to keep him company. We had dogs, chickens and ducks that roamed around the large garden and joined me on adventures. When I was five, I found a baby jackdaw that had fallen out of its nest. Bald and a little transparent, he was the ugliest creature imaginable, and I loved him completely. Mum named him Gerry, after Gerald Durrell, as she said my ability to find and bring home wildlife was reminiscent of his stories in *My Family and Other Animals*. Gerry came everywhere with me, and my days were spent chatting to my various animal friends with Gerry perched on top of my head. Once I started university and was living in cities, I never had any pets, it just didn't seem practical or possible, but as I sat with this little lamb on my knee I realised how much I had missed this contact.

After giving Yoda his last feed of the day, I got my hot water bottle, which had a soft fleecy cover, filled it with warm water, and placed it on his bed. I hoped this warmth would make him feel less alone. In the morning, as I fed Yoda his bottle, I worried about the conversations that I needed to have. Our landlord's response to my enquiry about keeping a lamb in the garage had been matter-of-fact and slightly enigmatic ('There has been far worse as a lamb in that shed'), and so I nervously waited for Lowrie. I desperately hoped he would allow Yoda to live in the field with his sheep – but what if he didn't? I didn't really have a plan B and felt that asking this favour was taking advantage of a neighbour's generosity.

As soon as I heard Lowrie's quad bike approaching I burst out of the house, Yoda close on my heels. Lowrie looked from me to the lamb and said, 'You poor girl, what have you done?'

Talking too fast, I tried to explain what had happened. Lowrie laughed kindly, interrupting my rambling to explain that at this time of year, everyone with a male caddy was trying to give them away. The trick was to be firm when you say no. Before I had a chance to ask, he said the lamb was welcome to live with his sheep and that there was plenty of grass for him, but he warned me not to get too attached. Desperate to show I wasn't some city type from down south, I assured him I would be very practical about this. I'd feed him and work to integrate him with the sheep. There would be no unnecessary cuddles. As Lowrie left he turned and asked if I'd named him yet.

'He's called Yoda.' I smiled.

He laughed and said, 'Good luck.'

It was a clear sunny day, so I sat outside with Yoda. Ina came round and said that Yoda was 'a lovely peerie fellow, a *lovely* peerie fellow', and offered to give him a bottle any time we were away. I gratefully accepted this kind offer, as I had been a bit worried about how to combine fieldwork trips off the island with feeding Yoda four bottles a day. Robbie joined us, said Yoda was a fine lamb, and then told us a story of a caddy he'd once known. When the lamb had been little, he would come into the house and sleep by the fire like a dog. Some months later, he'd joined a sheep flock on an uninhabited island, where he'd lived for many years. When the crofter had brought him home, this lamb, now a large Shetland ram with impressive horns, had immediately run into the house and taken his place by the fire as if he'd never left.

Wherever I went, Yoda followed a step or two

behind me. So I decided to take him for a walk along the ness. I reasoned that walking where his soon-to-be adoptive flock lived would be a good experience for him, to help him know he was a sheep.

The ness

When the Vikings came to Shetland they named the places they found. Names were often practical and descriptive, detailing geological features, events or activities. These names remain an important part of today's Shetland dialect, sometimes offering tantalising glimpses of how areas once were. When a derelict-looking expanse has '-bister', '-quoy' or 'swin-' as part of its name, you know that in the past, people farmed there. 'Ness', meaning 'headland', is a common place name in this land of rugged coastlines.

The ness was the place I walked, the place where I grew to know and fall in love with the Shetland landscape. Every day in this same place the experience was different, as more and more of its life was revealed to me. When I first arrived, its colours were muted, brown and mossy, interrupted by patches of brighter green in the wettest areas. Other than the sheep, and a few fulmar nestled into rock crevices or gliding on graceful wings, this land appeared vast and empty. Hints of others were revealed through shells, bones and scat, the remains of feasts. Barnacle-encrusted shells of various crab species and the empty carapace of giant sea urchins punctuated the rocky coastline. The regular appearance of the grotesque twisted corpses of ling with sharp teeth in gaping mouths told me that there must be several otters in the vicinity. I saw their tracks, their droppings, and found fur-coated areas of earth where they had been rolling, but for weeks the otters themselves remained elusive.

As I learned to sit and look, growing accustomed to the biting wind, I saw gulls (herring and black-backed) drop their underwater finds onto the rocks to break into the shells. I became increasingly aware of the attention of selkies. If I sat on a still day, it wouldn't be long before one silently appeared, watching, unblinking, then more and more would join them. Some would stretch their necks high out of the water, looking like they were bouncing on the spot to get a better view. They usually remained a few feet apart from one another, but sometimes they played, rolling corkscrews in the water, snorting and biting each other's necks. As I walked, these curious companions would often follow, disappearing beneath the waves, only to resurface parallel to the path I was walking.

One day, out of the corner of my eye, I saw a different movement. A large otter was making his way to shore, an orange butterfish dangling from his jaws. The brown of the otter's coat matched the colour of the thick forests of seaweed that the low tide had exposed. Had he not been moving, I could have been just feet away and known nothing of his presence. The sounds of tearing flesh and crunching bone travelled on the wind, and within minutes the otter returned to the water. A few feet out, he paused, looking back to the shore before, with arched back, he dived under the waves. Keeping my eye on the ripple that marked his decent, I crept forward, keeping low to the ground, to find a closer vantage point. The grey lichen-covered rock made a prickly and uncomfortable seat, but as the otter reappeared, closer to shore, I remained still. He swam a few feet and dived again, this time reappearing with another fish.

After this long-awaited sighting I regularly encountered otters as I explored the ness. Often I saw them hunting in the bay but occasionally I would meet them on land. Once, I found a sleeping otter, curled up in a hollow behind a large rock, its chest rising and falling with the rhythms of breath, fur moving with the breeze. It seemed small, and I wondered if it was a youngster. I crouched low, hoping to obscure my silhouette among the rocks, suspended in the moment, watching. After a few minutes the otter woke, stretched and started to roll, snapping its jaws as clouds of dust rose from the hollow. After stretching again, it paused, lifted its head, looking around, alert, before starting to rub its neck and cheeks along the rocks and seaweed. With one last look around, the otter defecated on the rock, which was already covered in scat, before slipping beneath the waves.

Every day, as I watched and learned, I saw land and sea merge, through the rhythms of life on the ness. I felt this otter must have been aware of my presence even as I remained hidden, with the wind blowing and carrying my scent. Were my more regular encounters with otters a result of them no longer taking such care to avoid me? I wondered if, as I walked, my presence was becoming a part of the place, that life on the ness was also learning to live with me.

Slowly, as they grew to trust me, Lowrie's sheep would come down off the hill to see if I had any food. I came to know several of the tamest ones well, giving them each names as I wrote about their antics in my fieldnotes. Starey Sheep was the moorit with the white stripe and bulging eyes, a close companion of Y-Face, the charcoal yowe. Four White Feet ... well, had four white feet, and the rest of her body was black apart from a white stripe in the centre of her face. Two other sheep were often with her, and I called them Pretty Pink Nose and V-Face, based on their markings. The amazing variety of colours and markings meant I was able to identify individual sheep in a way I had never been able to do with flocks I had met before.

One morning, I was sitting on a wall, Yoda at my feet, and noticed how spring had transformed the ness. Shades of brown had become green, and nestled among the new blades of grass were tiny purple flowers: spring squill. Only a few centimetres tall, beautiful but strong, they defiantly bloomed despite high winds and unseasonable hail showers. Bright pink flowers, toadflax-like in shape, clustered close to the stones. Where the longer grass grew, the first bog orchids were starting to emerge, some a rich purple, others a delicate, lace-woven pink and white. The air was heavy with a threat of rain, the opaque sky marbled grey with silver highlights. The sound of skylarks, carried with the wind from the heather hill, formed a constant background melody.

Closer, a wren sang. I would often see this tiny bird here, perched atop the highest stone, ready to dart, mouse-like, into a crevice, whenever I came too close.

Then a new sound rose, a haunting elongated wail that echoed through the landscape, radiating from hill, sea and sky so I could not tell from where it originated. Everything else fell silent as this sound, telling of unknown worlds, continued. The back of my neck prickled and goosebumps rose on my arms as another voice joined, and, lifting, the songs entwined around each other, enveloping me in their magic.

When I returned home, my eyes constantly scanning to see who had sung, Robbie was at the gate. 'Did you hear the rain goose?' he asked, and I realised I had been listening to the courting call of the red-throated diver. He told me a pair usually returned to each of the lochs in this area to breed, and they sing throughout their spring courtship. Every morning from then on, I listened, watching through binoculars as they swam parallel to one another, the red of their throats vivid against charcoal necks as they lifted their heads and sang. I grew to know this pair well, their shapes on the water a familiar sight throughout the summer.

The weather became more spring-like, and one morning as we walked together Yoda started bouncing, jumping high in the air, and clambering onto the lower parts of walls or rocks before hurling himself off once more. Lowrie's sheep stood at a distance, watching. A honey-coloured sheep with a very fluffy head moved forward a few paces. Yoda galloped over towards the flock and she darted back, appearing terrified of the lamb. As he approached the flock once more, a few sheep allowed him to come close, but the majority moved to get away from him, disappearing over the hill. Yoda ran happily full-speed back to me, seemingly unaffected by the flock's rejection of him. As I continued to walk, Yoda followed a few steps behind me. I fretted about how I could make him more sheep-like. Although he needed to sleep indoors at night until he was older and stronger, I had hoped he could spend his days in the sheep field. However, any time I placed him in the field, as soon as the sheep started to gather around him, he would decide he did not like sheep and would try to find his way back to me. These attempts were always successful, as the combination of his small size and the elderly nature of the walls and fences meant that minutes after hearing his panicked bleat he would reappear beside me.

As we drew closer to home, I noticed Yoda was walking to one side of me, rather than directly behind me as he usually did. My feet had left the well-worn sheep path that wound its way across the headland, but he remained steadfastly on it, moving in the same direction as me, but along a different path.

The garden

As the weeks became months, I was increasingly amazed by the generosity of our neighbours. They regularly gave us gifts of eggs, fish or other produce, always with a line such as 'We had a bit extra so thought you would like some,' or 'The hens are laying so much – we have too many.' I was left uncertain how to reciprocate.

We did not produce anything, we only had things we'd bought, and so it seemed unlikely that we would ever have extra that we needed to give away. I felt that buying something specifically to give wouldn't be right in this situation. But I really wanted to give something: I couldn't bear the thought of repaying kindness with rudeness.

My first thought was baking. I reasoned that I could easily make something that it would seem natural to share. Unfortunately, I had never baked before, and with most of my days on the mainland for fieldwork and hours of notes to write up every day, I had very little time to practise. My first attempts were too ugly, burnt or strange-tasting to give to anybody. As I improved slightly, by sticking to simple recipes and following instructions to the letter, I became more aware of the baking skills of islanders, who all seemed to be able to make scones, bannocks or fancies that were light and fluffy and seemingly without turning their kitchens into smoke-filled disaster zones. My own attempts seemed worse and worse in comparison. I worried that if I was to give people my own poor efforts it might look rude, like I was getting rid of baking rejects. My overthinking on this was causing me such anxiety that I decided to just get on with it and share my most recent attempt at cookies with Ina. They looked and smelled good but unfortunately,

I had not tried them before I offered her some. She bit into one; I could hear the sound of crunching. Although she smiled kindly, it seemed chewing it was requiring considerable effort. Once she had swallowed her mouthful, she said that it was lovely but she would save the rest for when she was home. As soon as she'd gone, I tried one. It was rock hard. I cried with disappointment and embarrassment, feeling like I had nothing to offer and didn't know how to be a good neighbour.

Once I stopped feeling sorry for myself, I decided I would work on growing some vegetables, hoping that later in the year I would be able to share the harvest. I went out and surveyed our garden. It was an absolute mess. Despite several dry days the grass remained waterlogged, and the ground sank a little wherever I put my feet, water filling the footprints I left behind. The areas that had once been used for growing were covered with a thick, tangled mat of dead grass, while a closer inspection revealed that this place had clearly been a feline toilet for some time. There would be a risk of exposure from a north wind, as nothing but a rickety wooden fence stood between the garden and the sea.

There were, however, bushes that could provide shelter from the south and east. Throughout the winter, I had watched as these bushes' bare, forlorn-looking branches were whipped by the wind and lashed with salt spray, and had begun to wonder if they were alive at all. But with the changing season, buds and fragile green shoots had begun to emerge. In the sheltered areas below, leaves grew up from the ground, straight and steady: daffodils and bluebells, Ina had told me. Not knowing what other potential might lie below winter ground, I decided to devote my efforts to the vegetable garden, a small flower garden, and a new path, and wait and see what grew in the other areas.

I started with the small area where I thought a flower bed might have been before. With the dry stone wall on one side and a large patch of rose bushes on the other, it seemed like a sheltered place. It was completely overgrown, so I set to work pulling up the grass. I found that if I yanked on a handful of stalks at a diagonal angle, they came out of the ground quite quickly, bringing with them clumps of wet earth. I dug, amazed how far their tangled roots stretched, enjoying the smell and feel of the earth on my fingers. In some patches, beneath the carpet of grass were small furled leaves, stretching up towards a sun they couldn't see. Intrigued, I cleared space around them, wanting to see what they would become. I unearthed a regular line of smooth stones that indicated this had indeed been a flower bed, and a faded garden-centre label confirming this. As I worked, Robbie came and leaned against the wall to chat. He said he thought there had been flowers and maybe some herbs in the area I was digging, and suggested I get to work on the vegetable patch soon if I wanted to get anything planted this year.

As I removed stones from the earth, placing them to one side, Robbie told me about a day when he'd been out walking and had found an unusual stone. It was not like any he had seen before on the isle, so he'd taken it to a geologist friend who'd confirmed it would have been from a ship's ballast. Ships would use rocks from their departure port to provide stability for their voyage, jettisoning these as they collected cargo, and, in doing so, creating enduring evidence of their journeys in the geology of places. He'd explained that because Whalsay had been an important port throughout history, as part of the Hanseatic trade route and as a regular stopping point for fishing vessels, the island's seabed contained many unusual stones. Robbie went away for a few minutes, returning with a large piece of flint, which he handed to me. He said that it too was likely off a ship that had come here long ago, and suggested I could keep it in the garden, or with the other stones I collected from the beach. I laughed and thanked him, aware of how visible I was as I walked along the ebb, examining rocks and bones and pocketing treasures like sea glass.

My arms were beginning to ache from digging, so I made myself a cup of tea and then fetched my packets of seeds and the small pots that would house them. I had chosen kale and cauliflower, both of which needed planting inside and would then be transferred into the garden later in the summer months. One by one, I filled the tiny pots with soil, placing a seed in the centre of each one and giving a little water before moving them into the porch. I then sprinkled some mint seeds into a larger pot by the front door.

The next morning was bright and sunny. The wind had moved to the south and it felt considerably warmer, although the local weather forecast confirmed it was just 10 degrees Celsius. The sun now rose high, and the song of the skylark carried from the hill, while the garden was alive with the sounds of sparrows and starlings. I began work on the vegetable patch by removing all the cat poo. Even though I was wearing rubber gloves and using a trowel, I hated this job, feeling unclean no matter how many times I washed my hands. Next I tackled the grass, but here it was far more stubborn, and my pulling technique from the day before had little effect. I used a fork to break the earth, cutting through several inches of matted, dead grass before reaching the soil below. Once I had removed all the visible grass, I set to work on what was underneath. The first half-metre below the surface was a tangle: extensive networks of fine grass roots; thick and stubborn dandelions reaching deeper than I could ever have imagined, and mysterious reddish-brown roots that I later discovered – when they continued to grow despite my best clearing efforts – were an invasion of mint. I worked for hours, feeling hot despite my breath being visible in the cold air, and slowly, I began to see a little progress as the area of bare soil grew.

I stopped for a moment, watching a neighbour's sheep as they made their way across the beach, their almost-identical white forms in a line as they followed in each other's footsteps. Except there were two darker sheep with them. I looked closer and saw Y-Face and Starey Sheep, Lowrie's sheep, with the wrong flock. Grabbing a bucket and some sheep nuts I headed towards them. The flock scattered, breaking formation and darting across the hill. I rattled the bucket loudly and Lowrie's two stopped and turned towards me. I rattled again, but they remained stationary, watching me. Unsure what to do next, I walked towards the gate of their field, still rattling the bucket, and hoping they would follow. When I reached the gate I opened it, standing back a little to give them room to pass through. They could see the sheep on the other side of the fence and clearly wanted to go through, but did not want to come any closer to me. I walked through the gate straight towards the flock, scattering sheep nuts around me. It worked, and the pair rejoined their flock. As I closed the gate behind me I felt a bit proud, happy that I had done something useful at last.

A little later, when I was back working in the garden, Lowrie came by on his quad bike, saying he had a couple of escaped sheep to round up. I said that I had herded them back to their flock. He thanked me and called me his helper. I was delighted.

Foal watch

May is the month when most Shetland pony foals are born, when the worst of the winter weather has passed and the new grass has begun to grow. I was trying to spend as much time as possible with pony breeders as they got to know the new additions to their studs, and was thrilled when Leona from the Robin's Brae stud had phoned to ask if I could help them with their foal watch on a day the whole family would be away from home.

Earlier in the spring I had met Leona and her brother, Irvine. They were the third generation of pony breeders in their family, and described growing up surrounded by animal lovers: 'You never knew what you would find opening the door – there might be a lamb in the porch.' Shetland ponies were always a part of their childhood, and they described helping out with tasks such as foaling and halter training from an early age.

As foaling time approached, the pregnant mares were placed in a field close to their house, and during the night the family took turns checking the horses. This level of attention was common among pony breeders, with many describing weeks of sleepless nights, made worth it by the joys of being there with their horses as the foals were born.

Shetland ponies are known to be good foalers, rarely needing assistance; however, complications can arise. On the phone the night before Leona had told me that only one foal had been born and that several of the mares were due. She'd said I should look out for mares showing signs of discomfort – rolling, pacing or frantically eating grass, any of these could be signs that labour was imminent. She'd described the signs that suggested a mare might be in trouble and had talked me through what I should do. She'd given me a list of phone numbers for the vet, family and neighbours, and had told me to help myself to the lasagne in the fridge. Although excited about the day ahead, I was reluctant to leave Yoda, who was still so little. Would he be lonely if I was away all day?

I went to visit the ponies in the further field first,

where I sat on a large stone overlooking the field. Shetland's distinct geology means there can be a striking difference in landscapes within a small area. Beneath the earth here was sandstone, which combined with the relatively flat topography created a fertile area, perfect for farming. The limited areas of cultivatable land in Shetland mean these most fertile regions have experienced near-constant human presence. Nineteenth-century crofthouses, formed from the stones of 2,000-year-old brochs (Iron-Age roundhouse towers), nestle beside the remains of mysterious Neolithic burnt mounds, where sheep and ponies continue to graze. This landscape is a tapestry, where the shapes of ancient walls live in the present, a connection to past farmers.

The green fields were separated by dry stone walls and the circular outlines of planticrubs stood at regular intervals. Although no longer used for agriculture, some of these crubs were still doing their job, as trees and shrubs, having found protection from the wind and hungry sheep, grew up to the height of the wall. The wind was brisk, and though I was sitting in the warmth of the sun, the lines and patterns along the horizon told me rain was on its way. Seven ponies, all heavily pregnant, stood with bums pointed towards the wind, most paying little attention to my intrusion into their field. A black-and-white mare lifted her head and made her way over to me, standing very close. Her nose was warm, and as she sniffed at my hands and face, the smell of her grassy breath brought back vivid memories of childhood days spent at riding stables. I took off my gloves and started to scratch her neck. Tufts of her winter coat flew with the breeze. She placed her head on my shoulder and started to lightly nibble at my jacket, moving with the rhythm of my scratching. This is something you regularly see between horses: they will stand and groom one another, and sometimes they extend this practice to the humans who take the time to groom them. Several of the other ponies had grown curious and gathered around, sniffing and nuzzling, their breath providing a little warmth from the cold wind.

I went inside to warm up. From the window I had a good view of the closest field where the ponies thought to be likely to foal imminently grazed. Jewel, a pretty brown-and-white mare, rolled on the ground and then made her way over towards the corner of the field, where she stood still, eyes closed. As another mare approached her, Jewel put her ears back and started to move away. My heart leaped: did this mean she was going to foal? Would I know what to do if she did? Remembering something Leona had said about some mares who were 'bursting to foal' that wouldn't go into labour if they thought someone was watching, I decided to stay inside, where I could see without being seen.

After about five minutes, Jewel turned, and slowly walked back to graze with the others. Happy that she was not going into labour, I went outside to sit with the ponies. I hoped the one foal, born just a few days ago, might come up to see me. Brown and white, with a spiky mane, long legs and knobbly knees, he was absolutely gorgeous. He seemed curious, watching me but staying close to his mum, moving around the field by her side and nursing regularly. At times he seemed to gain a little more confidence, stepping away from her and approaching the other mares. I watched as they immediately darted away from him, then stood looking between the foal and his mother. I was reminded of how the sheep responded to Yoda – maybe they thought I was his mother and might try to defend him? I decided to try keeping more of a distance from Yoda next time I was on the ness, to try to indicate that it was OK for the other sheep to approach him.

When the family returned, I described Jewel's behaviour, and Leona said it sounded like she might foal soon so she would keep an extra eye on her. Leona's husband had spent the day lambing and showed me pictures of the babies. It had been such a wet year that the lambs needed jackets. He showed me another picture of a line of lambs in bright orange waterproof coats. Because scent was so important for yowes and lambs to recognise each other, they were being kept inside together the first night, before their jackets were placed on. I felt my eyes well up thinking of my wee orphan lamb, alone at night with a hot water bottle, rejected by his mother and others of his kind. Trying to keep my composure, I smiled when Leona asked about Yoda, amazed that she knew about him. She said that they didn't have any caddies yet, but doubted they would get through a whole lambing season without at least one. Leona's father said that if you were quick you could sometimes get an orphaned lamb adopted by another yowe, describing how one year a yowe with no lamb had adopted a caddy and had even produced milk for the lamb. He paused for a moment, before telling a story about the local minister many years ago, a clever man but with little sense. He'd had a goat that had stopped producing milk so he'd asked the local crofters' advice. They'd told him he needed to get her covered. The next morning the community had found the minister had misunderstood the instruction, and instead of getting a billy goat to her, he had covered his goat in woolly jumpers. I laughed along with the family, not wanting to admit that until a few weeks ago I would also not have understood what was meant by 'covered'.

That evening, as I waited for the nine o'clock ferry

home, the light remained. The green of the land was highlighted in gold, the sea luminescent. Watching the boat slowly easing into dock, taking me home to my lamb after a day with Shetland ponies, I marvelled at how much my life had changed in just a few short months.

A Whalsay wedding

The next morning, Yoda appeared lacklustre. He drank his bottle, but then stood in the garden nibbling at some grass before lying down, eyes closed. This was such a contrast to how he normally behaved – galloping around at full speed – that I was instantly worried. I googled 'lethargic lamb what do I do?' and 'how to treat a sick lamb', quickly learning that *everything* can kill a pet lamb. He was making little grunts from the back of his throat and was grinding his teeth. Following advice from friends with sheep and what I read online, it seemed he might be suffering from bloat. While I waited for the vet to return my call, I cradled his head against my shoulder and placed my arm under his chest to keep him standing. His stomach did feel quite swollen, so I started to massage his tummy to try to get some of the gas out. His grunts intensified and, sure enough, out came a burp, closely followed by another. I continued, encouraged as gas regularly passed from both ends.

At the sound of Lowrie's quad bike I went over and asked his advice. Gently, he picked up Yoda, felt along his stomach and his legs, checking in his mouth and his ears, all of the time speaking to the lamb in soft tones: 'What ails de? What ails de?' He said that sometimes lambs are abandoned by their mums because the yowe senses something is wrong. My heart sank as I remembered Yoda's owner telling me how strange it was that the mum had abandoned the better lamb but had accepted the weaker-looking twin. Seeing the look on my face, he reassured me that there was still hope for Yoda. His eyes were bright and he still showed some curiosity – these were both good signs. Sometimes caddies just took a bit of a dip, and the vet would likely give him a vitamin injection, which would help him recover.

The vet called back and said they could see Yoda the next day, but until then I should reduce the amount of powder I was using in his bottles. Sometimes Shetland lambs respond badly to full-concentration yowe's milk replacement, and watered-down bottles might help. Bottles should be half strength and given twice as often until his appointment.

Today was the day of our neighbour's wedding and so far I had spent most of it in the shed with an ill lamb. I didn't want to leave Yoda, but felt that turning down such a kind invitation to stay home with a lamb might be unforgivably rude. Feeling that people might not understand our situation, Steve and I agreed that we would take it in turns to subtly drive home, to check on and feed Yoda, who now needed bottles every two hours. Not wanting to leave him in the garage, we brought his blankets and hot water bottle into the kitchen and made him a little bed in a cardboard box. I caught sight of myself in the mirror and realised I had a lot of work to do before I could leave for the wedding party – my skin and clothes were covered in lamb poo and my eyes were puffy and swollen from crying. Despite my efforts not to get too attached, I was, of course, completely in love with my small woolly friend, who bounced, *baa*-ed and followed me everywhere. The thought of losing him broke my heart.

When we arrived at the wedding, the party was in full swing. We chatted to friends and neighbours, and at around 8pm, I got the invitation I had been hoping for: the bride's father asked if I would like to visit the cookhouse. Across Shetland, different islands have their own distinct wedding traditions, and a central part of a Whalsay wedding is the mutton supper. Over the months I had lived on the island I had heard a little about this ritual. In the days before the nuptials, fourteen sheep are chosen, and on the wedding morning the cooking begins. The feast is always prepared in the same place, by the same group of men. Setting off to the cookhouse, I had little idea what to expect – many of the stories I had heard were vague on the detail, but apparently it was 'a bit like Dante's *Inferno*: all peat smoke and fiddle-playing'.

Stepping through the door, the heat and smell of cooking meat hit me like a physical force. Dominating the room was the largest fireplace I had ever seen, in which piles of peat burned, glowing bright in the dimly lit room. Sat atop the flames was a large silver beer keg, cut in half and with the number 2 painted on its wooden lid, and surrounding it, at various distances from the fire, were several more half-kegs, each with a painted number. On the wall behind the fireplace was a chalkboard with a list of numbers and times. Beside it there were photographs that looked like they went back several decades, all showing this room with groups of men cooking around the fire. I recognised some of the faces in the pictures as the same people who now sat in the chairs that circled this small room. There were about half a dozen men, some with tins of beer, others holding drams. An elderly man wearing a Fair Isle jumper stood up and walked over to the fire, lifting the lid of the pot to show us the contents. It was filled with large chunks of mutton, bubbling away with the heat of the fire. I asked what went into these pots and was told it was nothing but mutton, water, onion, salt and pepper. The flavour from these island-bred sheep is such that nothing else is needed.

We watched as two men removed the pot from the fire, placing it with the others by the hearth, and putting another one onto the fire, making a note on the board. The elderly man explained that there was a rotation system: pots boil above the fire, but the heat is such that they continue to cook when they are removed. The system for where to place them and the timings has been passed down through the generations. Once the meat reaches the hall, it joins cakes and bannocks, all baked by the community. 'Most places have forgotten how to do this now,' he said. 'Once, everywhere in Shetland would have cooked like this for a wedding, but we are the only place left that does it now.'

Accepting a dram, we sat a while. People came and went, the atmosphere relaxed and friendly. We were introduced as 'the new folk at Margaret and Willie's hoose', and everyone made us feel very welcome. Many of the guests came with a bottle of whisky and a glass. They would fill the glass and offer it to the person closest to them, who would take a sip and pass the glass back to its owner. The glass would then be topped up and passed to the next person, until everybody in the room had been offered a sip. In the weeks leading up to the wedding, Whalsay folk had told me many stories about visitors who had not understood the tradition and had drained the full glass each time it was offered, only to end up severely the worse for wear. Aware that later in the night I would be driving back and forth to Yoda, I only took tiny sips when offered a glass.

Conversation flowed, a blur of names and places with regular eruptions of laughter. Despite efforts to include us, and my longing to be a true part of such an event, I felt very much like we were on the outside looking in. A combination of accent, dialect and the island habit of referring to everybody by nicknames meant I understood little of what was being said, I didn't have the shared knowledge required to fully participate. Peat smoke filled the room with a thick haze, the fire crackled and pots sizzled, previous generations smiled down from the walls. It felt like community in the truest sense. Mutton and peat from the hill, cooked as part of a celebration where friends, families and neighbours joyfully continued an island tradition. The flow of visits, the easy conversation, laughter, nicknames and jokes, practised and perfected through years of shared lives, a dance of relating to each other, and to the island.

Each time I visited Yoda during the evening he

appeared weak, walking over to me on shaky legs and returning to his bed immediately after his feed. When I woke the next morning I approached the kitchen door with trepidation. I could hear no sound on the other side and I feared what I might find. As the door creaked open, Yoda's head popped up over the top of his cardboard box. He bleated and made his way over to me on shaky legs. The extra bottles had made quite the impression on his bladder and bowels, and he slipped several times in the mess he had created.

After I had wiped him down and given him his bottle, it was time to get the ferry and take him to the vet. I had borrowed a dog cage for the occasion to keep him safe and secure, as he would be in the car for several hours. The vet's first response was 'First time I've seen a lamb in a dog cage,' before asking a series of questions: Was he eating? Pooping? Able to stand? As I answered each question in the affirmative she looked increasingly puzzled, and so I awkwardly explained that he just didn't seem his usual self and I was worried about him. She examined him closely, and said she couldn't see anything very wrong with him, but gave him vitamin and penicillin injections and issued instructions to keep his bottles at their weaker concentration for a few days, before gradually increasing the quantity of milk powder again. Relieved, I started the drive home, wanting to catch the ferry in good time before the second night of the wedding.

Shetland weddings are a huge social occasion, and most weddings have a first and second night. The first night follows the ceremony and is usually a little more formal, with friends and family, while the second night is more of a big party for everyone in the surrounding area. The second-night party was taking place a ten-minute walk from our house, which would make going back and forth to Yoda a little easier, and as we'd be making the journey on foot, I would be able to have a dram.

It was a mild night with little wind and everybody sat outside chatting. Cans of beer were distributed at regular intervals, and most of the guests had brought their bottle of whisky and a glass to share. I had intended to go to Yoda without anybody noticing or knowing why I was gone, but when people asked about the lamb I found myself pouring out my woes and worries. To my surprise, everyone was genuinely very sympathetic, saying how attached you could get to caddies and sharing stories of their own experiences with lambs they had loved.

I was told about a lamb who had grown up to be much loved by the crofter who had bottle-fed her, but her continual noisy presence drove the rest of the family to distraction. Every attempt the family had made to sell her was thwarted. This reprieve seemed to have been extended to her descendants. The crofter's daughter told us that any brown sheep in the area was probably that caddy's great-great-great-granddaughter. An elderly woman told me about a caddy she'd been given to look after when she was seven years old. Her mum had made her give it back at the end of summer. She described how she could hear that lamb, recognising its bleat, distinct from the sounds of all the other sheep. She'd cried for weeks because she could hear him call but couldn't go to be with him. Another woman told me about a friend who had painted her caddies with zebra stripes the day before they were due to be sold, hoping this would prevent her dad taking them to the auction.

My love for my caddy, which I had thought might separate me further from the community, turned out to be a shared experience, making me feel more connected, even if most people's caddy experiences were from their childhoods. Caring for caddies is one of the ways the younger generations gain practical experience on the family croft, and learn about care, life and death. Long after the individual sheep are gone, the love for them remains, coming alive again in the telling and retelling of stories. Love, understanding and information flowed through these stories, and I came to understand these anecdotes as part of the landscape, of the social life between people and animals, across generations, part of the fabric of being in this place.

Knowing how Shetland stories carry instructions about island life, I paid attention to the animal stories people told me. I noticed that after I got Yoda, several people told me a story about 'the wife, fae sooth, who ended up with a hundred goats'. Somebody had moved to the isle and had adopted a goat – before long she had more and more. She didn't have the knowledge or experience to properly care for them, and her neighbours had to step in, eventually taking care of all the goats. This type of story is common: where somebody with little crofting experience naively takes on animals and then has to rely on the kindness of their neighbours to help them out when things inevitably go wrong. I was in no doubt that these kindly spoken stories carried a warning not to keep acquiring more animals, and I vowed to work even harder to teach Yoda to be a real sheep, determined not to leave behind a troublesome caddy when my fieldwork ended.

Over the following days, Yoda grew stronger. One day I walked with him along the ness, guiding him towards Lowrie's flock who were grazing in the distance. He walked steadily, the bounce back in his step. As we approached, Four White Feet and V-Face moved forward a few steps and, remembering the mares' responses to the foal at Robin's Brae, I retreated. Yoda stood for a moment before bounding back to me. I tried again, encouraging him forward towards the other sheep, and then trying to edge back without him noticing. Four White Feet looked from me to Yoda and took a step forward. Yoda stayed still, watching her. She sniffed him, and he then bleated in panic, running back to me at full speed while she walked back to rejoin her flock. I hoped she wouldn't lose interest in him, but for now it didn't matter that he was not acting like a sheep. I was just delighted he was well again.

Whenever I walked into their field with Yoda, the sheep would lift their heads, sniffing the air in a way that reminded me of deer or antelopes. I had never seen sheep do this before – usually sheep would graze until they saw me, pee, then run away. But now this flock was used to my presence, associated me with food, and seemed quite relaxed when I was in their field. I became more aware of my own body in relation to them, consciously moving in ways I hoped would communicate that it was OK to approach us, that they had permission to speak to Yoda. Four White Feet was becoming the boldest, moving away from the flock to see us. As she and Yoda got closer, I continued my practice of backing slowly away, hoping Yoda would not sense my departure. As I stepped back, Four White Feet moved forward. At first, whenever she sniffed him he would run away, but over time he allowed her to touch him, and started to sniff her in return. As her confidence in the situation grew, she would approach Yoda even when he was by my side and would follow him if he backed away. I asked Lowrie about her, if she had maybe been a caddy because she was so tame and trusting. He replied that she had never been a caddy but had been tame ever since she was a lamb. He told me she had had lambs in previous years, and must enjoy them if she was spending so much time with Yoda. 'I'll put her tae da ram when it is time, then she can have her own lamb next year.'

I went back to visit June, eager to hear more about her life with horses. When I knocked on her door there was a volley of barks as two large black Labradors hurled themselves against the glass door. June appeared, opening the door and shooing away the excited dogs. 'You shouldn't have knocked, it just confuses them,' she said, ushering me into the kitchen.

As soon as I had sat down, Vinnie, the younger of the two dogs, put his paws on my knees. In his mouth was a toy. He kept edging closer and closer towards me until his nose was nearly touching mine. June called him a daft bugger and said that he wanted to put the toy in my mouth and that I needed to tell him I didn't want that. I did so. Seemingly unconvinced by my refusal, Vinnie moved a few feet away, but kept watching me, edging closer, before finally giving up and joining the older dog who was now snoozing by the window.

Over a cup of tea, June described how as a child she had loved watched the hill ponies, keeping a diary of their actions, trying to learn all about them. She said that even after decades of working with ponies she was still learning, because ponies had so much to teach us. Where we sat at the table offered a spectacular view over the voe, where a small marina provided shelter for a number of fishing boats. June told me that everybody in the community knew each other's boats and this attention kept people safe at sea. She described how this sense of community is such an important part of Shetland life: people look out for one another and are always ready to help their neighbours.

We drove to visit her ponies, parking in front of a large area of hill park, and climbed over a gate and made our way up the hill. As we walked, June called out, letting the horses know she was there. After a moment, two horses appeared at the crest of the hill, then more and more ponies appeared as they made their way down the hill towards us. When they were about halfway down, the herd turned and cantered away. 'Whar ir you goin?' June called after them. She explained they were not used to two people coming into their field so we should sit a while and let them get used to my presence. Soon, the ponies appeared again, slowly making their way towards us, ears pricked, alert. June introduced the mare that reached us first as the matriarch of the herd, the one that the others listened to. June spoke softly, scratching the mare's neck, before standing up and walking back towards the food troughs. The herd followed, their hoofs squelching in the muddy ground. As the troughs were filled the ponies gathered around, jostling a little before settling to eat.

June pointed to a young skewbald mare. 'This is Hirta. She is about to move to Whalsay to find herself.' She explained that she liked Hirta, she was a nice pony, looked good, was intelligent and had very good breeding. She'd had a foal the previous year but June felt she hadn't enjoyed being a mum, and wasn't very good at it, so she wasn't going to make her a brood mare. 'You have got to watch them,' June emphasised. 'See how they respond to different situations and learn what they like.' She wanted her ponies to enjoy life and to have a purpose, so she was going to see if Hirta might enjoy being a riding pony, living on

Whalsay with Roselyn, who had had a lifetime experience with ponies.

We walked across the road to another field where two fillies stood, a bay and a piebald. 'I watch these two a lot an' see what they get up to,' June said. She was planning to sell the piebald, who was quickly becoming a disruptive influence, not allowing the bay to eat, just constantly annoying and distracting her, and chasing her about the field. June said this behaviour was causing the bay to become fidgety and flighty. She would keep the bay filly, who would join the herd of mares on the hill, where she could begin to calm down and learn from them.

Simmer dim

I got the last ferry home and it was nearing midnight as I walked out onto the ness, into the 'simmer dim.' Colours of sunset remained, the sky a patchwork of pale pinks, yellows, purples and striking duck-egg blue. Lightly rippling, the sea glowed like opal, gently splashing the rocky shore. It was not quite dark and the light had an unusual quality, seeming to radiate from land and sea to be reflected by the sky. Among the piping cries of oystercatchers and the haunting bubbling call of curlew, I noticed the new sound. For weeks,

Robbie and Lowrie had been anticipating the return of the tirrick (the Shetland name for the Arctic tern), talking about the dates they'd arrived in previous years and making predictions for this season. Arctic terns spend the winter months in Northern Europe and Africa, returning to coastal areas of Britain in spring.

I walked down to the beach. The terns circled above, their shrill cries filling the still air. Despite me keeping my distance from their nesting area, the sound from the colony rose to a piercing shriek. Three birds separated from the others, flying towards me. Directly above my head they stopped, hovering on silver wings, suspended. They looked so delicate, beautiful, almost angelic, yet even in the fading light their beaks appeared treacherous and their cry sent shivers down my spine.

I turned towards the ness, the beauty of the midnight light with its feeling of magic bringing alive the landscape's ephemeral, intangible qualities. It reminded me of the words of Neil M. Gunn:

> Many are susceptible to the peculiar power of the twilight, particularly in lonely places. For me it can evoke figures I knew as a boy; tranced hunting moments at the back of woods, in a glade, eyes staring at cleft rock, ears hearkening for the inaudible. Two orders of being, the visible and the invisible, pause on the doorstep of

this grey hour, and which is going to advance upon you you hardly know.

In this stillness, I felt worlds combine. It used to be common knowledge that Shetland is inhabited by trows. These little people stand just a couple of feet tall, and are described as hideously ugly. They live underground, usually below rounded hillocks called knowes. After dark, trows would cause all sorts of mischief about the croft. They might milk the cow, take food from the kitchen, or sneak into the house to warm themselves by the fire. Though they are most often invisible, known only through the results of their actions, some tales tell of face-to-face encounters. Where, lit by the moon, or the last rays of the sun, strange shapes emerge from the landscape, tempting humans to their underground homes. Trows are said to be enchanted by music, and it was often human musicians that were invited into these trowie knowes. Some of Shetland's best-known fiddle tunes bear the names of the trows said to have composed them. I sat, enjoying the moment, wondering about all those unseen who may share our world.

Although my first thoughts were of the folk stories I'd heard, it was more than that that made the night's walk magical. As I sat watching the light from the glowing land fade, listening to the curlew, Lowrie's sheep made their way slowly down to the beach and started to eat the seaweed. Soon these sheep would be sheared, their wool taken, spun and made into Shetland ganseys. In autumn, yowes would go to the ram and older wethers would become mutton, feeding families who have lived here for generations. In spring, the cycle would begin anew, as lambs would join the flock, and people and animals would continue to live together, living as part of this beautiful landscape. I felt connected to the ebb and flow of life here, happy be part of this place.

4

FOULA

As we walked across the runway towards the tiny blue plane, I turned to Steve, hoping for some reassurance about the impending flight. Although I had been looking forward to the journey, until this point I hadn't realised exactly how small the islander planes actually were. Before I could voice my concerns, the pilot opened the door and asked us to take our seats and fasten our harnesses. If anything, the aircraft seemed even smaller inside: eight seats tightly packed together, the lights and dials in the cockpit almost within reach. Suddenly, the whole plane started to shake and vibrate into life as the engines began their deafening roar. Watching the propellers whirr, my eyes were continually drawn to the wing, which looked like a patchwork of metal, riveted together and attached to the body of the aircraft. I reasoned to myself that all planes are somehow stapled together, it is just that you don't usually see the joins.

We trundled and bounced along the runway. I expected we would turn, build up some speed, and take off in the other direction, but to my surprise I realised the wheels had already left the tarmac and we were airborne. I felt the plane lift and lurch with the gusts of wind, the engine sound rising to a higher pitch, and watched as the pilot worked with the dials, speaking into his headset. Although I could not make out his words, his relaxed tone of voice helped reassure me that this bumpy journey was normal. Within minutes the plane levelled off, our cruising altitude so low that details of the landscape below were clearly visible. I watched the scene unfold, miles of rugged hill, dotted with small crofts and patches of green. We traced the shoreline, where red cliffs were continually splashed by white-crested waves, their motion echoing the feel of the wind against the plane. As we turned sharply, heading out to sea, I recognised four tiny dots on the cliff-lined peninsula as some Shetland ponies, and marvelled at their ability to live as part of such a wild landscape.

Five peaks loomed ahead, the only land visible in this vast ocean, the edge of the world. Lying around 20 miles off the Shetland mainland, and with only around thirty residents, Foula is one of Britain's most remote places. The island had been a presence from the moment I arrived in Shetland. Whenever I looked out over the Atlantic, my attention and imagination were often drawn to Foula's mist-shrouded hills, at times appearing tantalisingly close, on other days made invisible by the weather.

The plane juddered and the drone of the engine changed as we descended, lower and lower, the froth of the waves visible, but no sign of a place to land. Tilting at an alarming angle, with a few sickening lurches we turned, making a straight path towards the hills. I could see a long valley, green and empty apart from a few lonely-looking crofthouses and a single strip of tarmac that I realised must be the airport. Seemingly with no reduction in speed, lilting slightly, the plane hurtled in to land, bouncing several times before making its final stop, the engine falling silent and the propellers slowing until they were still.

After barely a moment to catch my breath, the door opened and we were greeted enthusiastically by Fran, a petite young woman dressed in leggings, wellies and a Fair Isle jumper. She introduced herself as the owner of the house we'd be staying in, and she said she would give us a lift there as soon as she had helped some folk onto the plane. We walked over to a small shelter by the side of the runway and watched the island prepare for the plane's departure. A fire engine was stationary at the end of the runway, and a woman in fluorescent overalls took a reading from the small weather station while keeping an eye on a flock of sheep, ready to shoo them away should they stray onto the runway. Boxes were loaded onto the plane and the small group said their goodbyes as the doors closed behind them. I noticed I was standing next to a basket filled with long pieces of wood; a handwritten sign taped to the basket read: BONXIE STICKS £1. Next to them was a small pile of business cards advertising Robert's Gift Shop, located at the school. Fran laughed when she saw what I was holding, and said that Robert was a skilled entrepreneur and it was well worth a visit to his shop. I was a little baffled as I had been told the island had no shop, and Fran explained that ten-year-old Robert, the school's only pupil, created and sold items to visitors, and the income from this endeavour funded some additional equipment for the school. That year they'd bought iPads.

We drove along the only road, a 2-mile stretch of rough-surfaced tarmac, and as we passed people Fran would stop the car for a chat, introducing me and telling them about my research, before going on to discuss island matters. I listened as conversations flowed: where ponies had been seen, an impending sheep roundup, and the likelihood of mist the following day. While we drove, Fran spoke animatedly about her croft and her sheep, and her hopes that school numbers would increase so that when her wee boy was old enough to start there would be other children in his class. Her love for her island home radiated from her every word and gesture.

After driving for a few minutes, we reached the end of the island. The road became a gravel track descending towards a sprawling crofthouse nestled between hill and sea. After helping us unpack, Fran said that she was sure to see us around and to give her a shout if we needed anything. The cottage didn't have a phone line, but she described some places we could walk to for mobile signal, and in an emergency we could go along to the nearest house – she pointed back along to the road – to use their phone. As her car departed, and I stood surrounded by the low melodic hum of the wind, an intense awareness of our isolation struck me.

The hill, its sharp peaks silhouetted against a silver sky, seemed unnaturally present, uncanny almost, dominating the landscape and drawing me to it. I walked along the coast, towards the hill, into a world of colour and motion. Tiny purple orchids, squill, buttercups and daisies formed an ornate carpet, with short stems, petals close to the ground. Sheep and lambs roamed, their fleeces gold, brown, charcoal and white, and many combinations in between. Small pieces of their wool, caught in the grass, added colour to the dance of bog cotton, as it moved with ever-present wind.

On one side the hill towered above me as I lay on my stomach, tentatively moving across a narrow peninsula, its sloping side giving the sickening feeling of falling, down towards the waves far below. Deep gurgling echoes, seeming to come from the very land itself, told of caves carved out from the rock beneath me. Inch by inch I moved, until I was looking back to where the side of the hill gave way to vertical cliff. The red sandstone blazed in the light of the setting sun, long shadows stretched across its rugged face, a patchwork of weathered cracks and crevices, many of which provided homes to pairs of fulmar, whose cackling call echoed between rock, sea and sky. Guillemot and razorbill inhabited the ledges closest to the water, and the air was filled with the sharp tang of guano. Suddenly, from the fringe of thrift that marked the edge of land, a face appeared. A puffin, followed immediately by another. I held my breath as they came close, noticing but not avoiding me, I could see the detail of their feathers, the startling colour of their bills and feet. They shuffled past and in a moment they were gone. I lay spellbound as more and more puffins appeared, emerging from a network of hidden burrows. Some carried grass in their bills, while the scuffling sounds and clouds of dust carried on the wind suggested further excavation and nest improvement. A pair rubbed bills, a dance of familiarity, an act of remembering. Just a few weeks ago these two would have been apart, separate in a large ocean, before meeting again, as they would every summer, at the same island burrow.

Every year, since before the history of this island was written, when spring eases towards summer, seabirds in their thousands come to these shores to raise chicks, before returning to the ocean. This regular abundance became a staple in island diets. Men attached to ropes would make the breath-taking journey down the cliffs to collect birds and eggs, risking their lives to supplement what could be cultivated in the small areas of fertile land. Today, Foula's residents continue to pay close attention to their avian neighbours, watching their behaviours and nesting patterns, counting breeding pairs and chicks, and sharing these observations with conservation organisations to help build a picture of seabird health across Britain. The entire island is a designated Special Protection Area for seabirds, and the cliffs have the additional status of Site of Special Scientific Interest due to the immense seabird cities they house. This combined effort, of international designation and local attention, works to ensure these ocean voyagers always have this safe place to return to.

The name Foula comes from the Old Norse *Fugla-ey*: Bird Island. I was here in their home, feeling this world of time, season and stone. A gust of wind, stronger and more insistent than those that had come before, broke the spell, reminding me of my precarious position, and I eased myself back to more solid ground. Sunset filled the air, infusing the sea haze with a warm glow, while the pewter sea was streaked pink, and curious selkies watched me make my way home.

Post office

I followed the arrow on a hand-painted sign down a track to a small cluster of houses. A piebald stallion pranced, watchful, his mane whipped by the wind. In the next field a grey mare and a chestnut foal stood, ears pricked, while a small brown pony approached the gate. Fish boxes, in their new role as plant pots, overflowed with yellow and red nasturtiums, and on the wall of the old stone crofthouse was a large red POST OFFICE sign. The door to the porch was open, and inside this tiny room was a long wooden counter, stacked with leaflets, envelopes and stationery. Behind the counter stood Sheila. I guessed she was in her sixties or seventies, her long grey hair tied back in a ponytail. She was silent, watching me as I introduced myself and explained a little about my research. She said she had heard about my project and would be happy to be involved, adding that she would be here until it was time to close the post office, so there was plenty time to talk. I marvelled at the size of the post office, impressed that it existed at all in such a small community, and I asked if could take her picture. She agreed pleasantly enough, but in the slightly resigned manner of somebody who has been asked this many times. I realised, feeling a little guilty, that probably everybody wanted a picture of Britain's most remote post office. I hastily changed the subject to ponies, saying that I had not seen many since I'd arrived.

'Most of our ponies are out there,' Sheila told me, gesturing behind her, towards the hill. She explained that even though she didn't go out to see the ponies every day, she could be fairly sure where they were. As she went about her daily life, rounding up sheep, leading guided walks, or participating in bird counts, she'd notice where the ponies were and what they were doing. Through this attention she had gained a deep knowledge of the preferences, friendships and habits of her ponies. She described how over time she'd realised that older mares – even from different herds – would often start to spend time together. In the past, these groups of mares would often successfully avoid the stallion, choosing not to allow themselves to get in foal, but even now that there is no stallion on the hill the 'OAPs' still formed their own group.

She had learned to interpret the herd's behaviours in relation to weather and season, adjusting the rhythms of her own life to lessons from the hill. Seeing where ponies chose to shelter gave clues about approaching bad weather – more accurate than official weather forecasts, which were often too general to account for the particularities of a small island surrounded by the vast Atlantic. In summer, when she saw ponies running, prancing, shaking their tails and heading to the highest parts of the hill, then she knew it was a good day to round up the sheep. The ponies were moving to get out of the way of dense midge clouds, which also bothered the sheep. This meant the flock would be happy to be herded down towards the croft, where the wind coming in off the sea would likely disperse the midges somewhat.

If some days had passed and a particular pony had not been seen, she would ask around to see if anybody else knew where they were. If none of her neighbours had seen the pony recently then she would go to the hill to look for them. In most cases the ponies would be found fairly quickly in the places where they were expected to be. She spoke sadly about times when a pony has vanished, never to be seen again. 'In your heart you might know they are gone, lost over the cliff, but you still look, still hope.' She was quiet for a moment, her eyes looking past me, out the door and towards the sea. 'It is rare though,' she said. 'Most of the time ponies know how to live on the hill, and the benefits they get, the freedom and opportunity to live a natural life, outweigh the risks.'

As we stepped outside into the sunshine I asked Sheila when she had begun pony breeding. 'Each year we name foals by letter of the alphabet, so the first year all names started with the letter A, and then B, and so on. And now we have reached M for the second time.' As I hastily tried to do the maths, she said she had loved horses all her life, and so, when she and her husband Jim were looking to expand their crofting activities, it seemed like the natural thing to do. 'Here,' she gestured around her, 'is where my grandfather kept ponies, the exact same place.' We approached the mare and foal, the mare standing a few paces back, eying me warily, while the foal stepped forward to greet us. Sheila laughed and said the mare could be a little grumpy but had good bloodlines and was a fantastic mother, consistently producing good foals and teaching them well.

'I only breed now for the love of it,' she said. 'To put my knowledge of horses into practice.' She described how over the years she had learned which mares and stallions combined well, and what traits she valued so she now had a herd of ponies that she really liked, and the experience to breed more. The only problem was the market. A reduced demand for ponies over the last decade had resulted in there being many more foals bred than would sell. So Sheila had drastically reduced the number of ponies she bred. The chestnut foal was her only one this year. 'It's heartbreaking,' she said, 'but my responsibility is to the ponies. I only breed what I am happy to keep, then, whatever happens at the sale, they still have a home.'

In the afternoon, Steve and I walked to visit Robert's Gift Shop, which opened at school closing time. With green wooden walls and red roof, the school is one of the newest buildings on the island. Inside was bright and airy with small tables and chairs and walls filled with photographs and pupils' artwork, just as you would see in any primary school. The only difference was that Robert was this school's only pupil. He placed his wares on a table for us to examine: bookmarks he had made with pressed flowers, magnets with ponies or puffins, and tea towels printed with Robert's drawings of Foula through the seasons. Fran, who works at the school, and the headteacher chatted to us as we browsed. When they discovered that Steve was a film-maker they became more interested, asking if we could maybe come back the next day to give Robert a lesson in film-making.

The next morning when we arrived at the school, Robert and two teachers were sat around one of the small tables, ready for Steve's lesson. They had the new iPads out and asked if Steve could use these to help Robert to film and edit a video. As they discussed possible film topics and technical details, my eyes wandered across the walls. There were photographs of groups of children on various beaches and hills, smiling in their hats and knitted jumpers. Cut-out paper headings on colourful borders explained that these were trips to Fetlar and Fair Isle. One of the teachers told me that the small island schools, many of which have just one or two pupils, will regularly get together for trips to each other's islands, giving the children a chance to socialise.

Robert had decided to make a video about the school's polycrub. Growing anything in Shetland is a challenge as salt spray carried on strong winds can kill even the hardiest plants unless adequate shelter is provided. Just as stone planticrubs were a way for islanders to protect seedlings from weather, today, polycrubs perform the same function. Made from recycled piping from salmon cages and reinforced polycarbonate, these structures are designed to withstand winds in excess of 100 miles per hour. Robert moved slowly, filming the interior of the polycrub, which was filled with plants: pumpkins, peas, strawberries and hanging baskets overflowing with tropical-looking flowers. Narrating for the video, Robert explained that there was a place in the crub available for any member of the community who wanted one. The school had a small patch, and they were hoping that some of the produce could be used for one of their 'Fancy Friday' meals, where once a week the whole school ate lunch together, complete with nice plates, tablecloths and napkins.

After the lesson we walked back to the cottage. The wind was considerably colder than it had been just a few hours earlier, and there was a haze in the distance. I became aware of the horizon, the haze building, moving closer, the world around us shrinking, closing in. The sky lowered to meet the hill. Tendrils of mist travelled on the wind, seeking, reaching, grasping. A sudden chill as they passed, through us and by us, each with another close behind. Soon we were enveloped, caught in the flow of this opaque river. Ghostly shapes of seagulls and sheep appeared then evaporated before my eyes. Then I could only see a few steps ahead, hills and houses obscured. I thought of the times I had looked out to sea to find Foula had disappeared, and I knew that in this moment, from the mainland we were invisible. Adrift on an island floating in a cloud. I heard a rasping sound, followed by a cluck: a bonxie was nearby. I looked around and saw its outline, watching us through the swirling mist.

Since arriving in Foula, I had been aware of bon-xies' attention, their watchful presence, the eyes of the hills, and wondered why they don't feature in fireside tales the way that seals and others who dwell in this landscape do. They feel so knowing, otherworldly, and as this one called out again, I wondered if it was speaking to us, to another bird, or to the very air itself.

Guided walk

The next morning, I met Sheila for a guided walk. The mist had lifted, the hills newly washed in the sun. Sheila led me along a narrow path towards a white house. The sea was calm, deep blue beneath dancing diamonds of sunlight on water. Lupins and foxgloves nestled within of a network of walls, while the tallest of the red-hot pokers stretched up beyond the shelter of the stones, swaying slightly in the warm breeze.

'This was the kale yard,' she said. 'There would have only been flowers around the edges, most of the area was used to grow vegetables.' She pointed to three sycamore trees. The largest, with branches twisted into shapes beneath its leaves, stood only a few feet above the walls. 'My grandfather planted that big one and my dad planted that,' she said, pointing to each tree in turn, 'and I planted this one.' We crossed a wooden bridge over a small burn, and I noticed three large semicircular stones propped up against the wall, and realised they were millstones. Sheila explained that during the Bronze Age, large trough querns were used for grinding grain to produce flour. In Foula this practice continued until a few hundred years ago. 'The only querns found on the island were all broken, and it is said the laird broke them to stop the crofters making their own flour. This forced them to use the laird's mill, which required payment of a tax, further increasing their indebtedness to the landowner.'

The path wound its way uphill, towards the cliffs, the red rock striking against the green grass and blue sky. 'This is where I take folk to see norries,' Sheila said, explaining that in Shetland dialect puffins are known as tammie norries. She looked out to sea. 'You know it really is spring when they come back.' She described the joy of returning birds, the noise and bustle after a long winter. I could see some fulmar pairs huddled on rocky ledges, patches of guano indicating the presence of others, a distant call of kittiwake, but other than that, the place appeared empty. Sheila said it didn't sound, smell or feel like a seabird cliff anymore. Every year she did seabird counts and every year the numbers were lower, with startling decreases recently. She attributed much of the decline to over-fishing and its resulting sand eel depletion. These tiny fish are the main source of food for most of Shetland's seabirds, and declines force birds to journey further out to sea, exhausting them and increasing the likelihood of them abandoning their nests. A changing climate will only make it harder for sand eels and seabirds to find balance again, as warming oceans and changing distributions further disrupt the ties between species. 'No norries today,' Sheila said sadly. This year had been far worse than any she had known. Several years before, thousands of seabirds had died over winter, thought to be as a result of severe storms far out at sea. Identification rings from perished birds suggested that many were from Shetland populations, and now the quietening cliffs seemed to confirm this.

We turned inland, past the airstrip, towards the hills. The sky filled with the sounds of skylark and curlew, while wheatear called, hopping from rock to rock, joining us on our journey. As we passed silently, watching bonxies, I asked Sheila why there were so few of these birds in Shetland stories. She said that the high numbers of bonxies on the island were relatively recent, so this might explain their absence from stories, but that seabirds in general don't feature much in the folklore, which is surprising given how important they have always been for life here. She said that there are a lot of stories in Foula about njuggles, characters from Shetland folklore similar to Scottish kelpies. She described how island stories say njuggles would take up residence under watermills, preventing the wheel from turning. Njuggles could be dangerous neighbours, causing harm and misfortune, and were notorious for stealing items from their human neighbours, especially around Christmastime.

Before long, the valley opened out to reveal the sea on the other side of the island. A single interpretive board, incongruous next to such a dramatic vista, told us we were at Da Sneck Ida Smaalie, a 100-foot-deep rock fault cut into the cliff. We stood looking into this sheer-sided corridor of rock as it stretched towards the sea. Any words, exclamations of how amazing and beautiful it was, would sound hollow, hanging in the air, mocked by the wonder of this place, so I was silent. Near the top of the rock, there were patches of grass and flowers, sea pink clinging to life along tiny ledges, but further in it grew dark and cavernlike. Trickles of water ran down the moss-covered walls, echoing as they splashed into the pool far below. Individual drops, caught by the sun, transformed into flowing drops of light: will-o'-the-wisp.

The feeling of energy, of otherworldly magic, remained with me as we walked around the length of the sneck. Sheila pointed to a ridge below us, tracing with her finger the path the sheep would take when they were brought in from the hill. 'The sheep know the way,' she said, watching a small flock moving in the distance. 'We just guide them when it is time.' When they are young, lambs live at the croft, getting plenty of feed and learning to work with the dogs. It is only when their first winter has passed that they join the flock on the hill, where the older yowes teach them the ways to live in this place. Over time, they become hefted, for ever connected to the landscape.

I sat by the cliff edge, looking out into the blue of sea and sky, silver sunlight dancing on the surface of the water the only motion in the expanse. Tremulous notes rose from the sea below, filling the air with a melody familiar yet strange. It was the wild wind howling on a stormy night, yet softer too – glass bottles singing in a summer breeze. 'Selkies,' Sheila said quietly, and I suddenly understood I was listening to the song of the seals.

I felt the presence of time, the ancient breed of sheep roaming the hills, the people who nurture and understand them, the birds, ocean and seals, eternal, ordinary and magical. I noticed my body and the feeling of flow between me and the surrounding world, a surprising lack of tension. Until I'd come to Shetland, I had not realised how much stress had become part of me. I perhaps hadn't recognised it as anxiety or worry, just an inevitable franticness that came from the inescapable cycle of low-paid temporary jobs and the continual looming threat of unemployment. My life had been dominated by work and job applications, my spare time filled with voluntary work to improve my CV, in the hope of securing a more permanent position. The busyness of uncertainty had affected my body and mind, aches from the constant tension in neck and jaw, whirling thoughts preventing sleep, tears at unexpected times. It was only when I'd arrived in Shetland, as the initial feelings of wonder and excitement had subsided, as I had begun to adjust with the flows of island life, that I'd felt an easing, a lightening in my body. Worry's presence had only become visible through its absence. Walking for me, rather than a means to a destination with my head filled with lists and fears, had become a time of peace, the beginning of opening up to the world, which I felt opening to me in response, offering a possibility of further connection.

Although I was new to Shetland, I felt at home here, in a wind filled with selkie song. I wondered why some places affect us this way – what is it that changes a fleeting encounter into a lasting memory? A moment that changes us? To make a memory the brain and body interpret information: make imprints, or the possibility of new pathways as we change in relation to the worlds we experience. Yet not all encounters have this effect. I thought about feeling the silent Glasgow wind, the journey that had led me back here, which seemed simultaneously unlikely but inevitable. I wondered what would have been if I had not had this moment, or had ignored it, dismissing the possibility that the wind might speak to me. I thought about city life. Although there was much I'd enjoyed about it, it had never been home, and, without realising it, I'd been losing touch, fraying the connection between me and the natural world I loved. Is it inevitable that the built environment changes our perspective and relationships in this way? Or is there a magic of city streets that allows some to have a connection, a sense of belonging? I knew that for me, here was where I now needed to be. I heard a distant bleat, and saw the fleeting movement of the flock on the hill, and wondered how the sheep and land remembered. The encounters that altered their pathways, the imprints that changed them, became part of their imagination, part of their story.

Emily and the hill

The next morning, I visited Emily to meet her ponies. As I approached the house, a group of sheep and lambs dashed towards me, stopping a few feet away, staring. When I called, 'Kid! Kid! Kid!' they came a few steps closer, before turning and disappearing around the side of the house, *baa*-ing loudly. A long, low-roofed stone byre stood next to the house, and the remains of an old car provided shelter for bags of animal feed. Emily explained that it was difficult to remove large items from the island, as the ferry had limited capacity, and so islanders had learned to make good use of what others may consider rubbish. The car would never drive again but it did the job of a storage shed perfectly.

We went around the house to a large field and immediately a blue roan pony walked over to us. Emily stretched out her hand and the mare nuzzled her. 'This is Misty. She is very friendly,' she said. 'Maybe a little too friendly,' she added, as Misty turned around and started backing into me. 'She wants you to scratch her rump,' Emily said, laughing, and I dutifully obliged. We walked through the field, Emily introducing each pony and telling me a little about them. She lifted a chestnut mare's mane to reveal two small beads braided into the hair. This pony looked so similar to another island pony. I scratched the mare's neck, and she moved her nose in towards my arm and then rested her head on my shoulder. Emily was visibly taken aback. 'She is never like that with anybody except me – never usually even speaks to a stranger.' I was delighted: I've often found that when people's dogs and ponies show that they like me, especially if they are usually nervous of strangers, then their owners are more inclined to trust me. Whether because of this, or just because conversation flowed easier with time, the details Emily shared about each horse moved on from the particulars of breeding and prizes won to include more about their shared lives and her love for them.

We stepped into a large field, where long grass and wildflowers swayed in the breeze, and two chestnut-and-white foals chased each other in circles as their mothers grazed. We crouched down and within moments the foals came over with soft noses and in-quisitive eyes. They were starting to lose their foal coat, leaving patches of darker hair around their eyes and mouths, giving them a rather comical look. At first glance, they had looked similar in height, bone and colour but as Emily told me about them, I began to see the differences. One she said had definite stal-lion potential. She traced the lines of his body in the air as she described his conformation, moving her own body in relation to his as she drew my attention towards the ways he lifted his feet and his head as he trotted. She said she liked the other foal – he was a good foal, nice temperament, and no imperfections, but he just didn't have that certain 'something' that the first foal had.

Emily stroked their noses and ran her hands along their legs, picking up their feet, while they nuzzled in, gently nibbling her jacket, before tearing off around the field, chasing each other again. 'I spend a lot of time with my foals,' Emily said, describing how touching their noses and feet got them used to the contact they would need when they were older, such as halters and hoof trimming. During their first winter they got extra feed and she kept a close eye on them during periods of bad weather. Her ponies would usually spend time down at the croft until they were about four. Through these practices, ponies become used to contact and learn to associate the croft with food, care and safety. I asked Emily when she brought pregnant mares down from the hill ready for foaling and she replied, 'I don't. It's the ponies who choose when to come down, and they know the right time.' While living up on the hill, ponies will often choose to return to the croft: to visit other members of their herd; to get a little extra feed, or if they have fallen ill. Emily said that she trusted the animals' intelligence and instincts to know when to come.

I began to realise that how these crofters in Foula work with their animals embodies the ideals of autonomy and adaptability that Shetland pony breeders value. For most of their lives the ponies live independently on the hill. Their owners, trusting their intelligence, allow them to thrive in their herds with minimal human intervention. Although at first glance this may seem like a very hands-off form of animal husbandry, in practice it takes a lot of time and knowledge. It is not a case of just setting animals loose on the hill and expecting them to survive. Ponies' early years are characterised by intensive human contact, and Sheila and Emily would never have put an animal out on the hill unless they'd felt they had the knowledge and skills to thrive out there. They needed to trust that each pony had the sense to live as part of the hill herd, but also that they considered the croft a safe place they could return to. Although they did not often go into the hill to tend to their ponies, their everyday attention, through island life, was connected to the lives of their ponies. Their own landscape perceptions merged with their knowledge of ponies and place, an art and an act of noticing. This attention extends from breeders to other members of the community, and so ponies become part of the conversation and social life of this island.

After I left Emily's house I walked up to the hill, to look for ponies. The heather was thick and wiry underfoot – it would be some time before the first purple blossoms emerged. Lines where peat had been cut years before now sank in on themselves as they wound around the side of the hill. I heard a *cluck*, followed by a *swoosh*. A bonxie had swooped, missing my head by inches. Another came, and then another. I remembered Robert's bonxie sticks and realised I might have wandered into the hill a little unprepared. I saw a movement, and a chick, creamy yellow, with long legs, looking rather like a tiny ostrich, dashed out from behind a tussock and disappeared under a peat bank. Several bonxies circled overhead, occasionally swooping low towards me, a watchful warning that I was in their place and should move on. Heeding their advice, stooping low, I walked up the hill again, towards a ridge. In the distance, I saw a herd of ponies, their coats – chestnut, black, grey, roan – gleaming in the sun, some colour in this otherwise barren hill. I watched as they grazed, some mares looking up occasionally, checking around them before turning their attention back to finding the best blades of grass among the heather. They moved as one, slowly across the hill, as thousands had done here before them, in this place of wind and birds. I felt the history and presence of the hill, and I suddenly understood that this landscape was an active participant in domestication relationships as much as the people and ponies were.

It is these places that have created and sustained ponies. Over centuries, the ponies have lived as part of this landscape, and people have learned as they live with them. Adaptability, one of the most valued breed characteristics, developed in relation to this landscape. Living on the hill, ponies needed to travel large distances over difficult terrain to find food and use judgement about where to go in bad weather. Movement style, surefootedness and strength, along with independence, intelligence and adaptability developed from these relationships with place. Many pony breeders described how after periods of intensive work, such as halter training, ponies need some time on the hill to relax and process what they have learned. They spoke of the hill as a natural environment for them, somewhere they could relax but also where they needed to keep their wits about them as they learned to live as part of a herd. In this way, they learned the skills needed to interact effectively with humans while also being given the freedom to live their own lives out on the hill. This balance between working with humans while still having freedom was a feature of stories of the hill. Breeders are not wishing for a return to the days when the majority of hill ponies were rarely handled or worked with, but equally they are reluctant to dominate too much of their ponies' lives.

Thom van Dooren, in his book *Flight Ways,* describes the importance of understanding that 'places are interwoven with and embedded in broader histories and systems of meaning through ongoing, embodied, and inter-subjective practices of "place-making". He emphasises that these storied places are not only something that humans experience, but that non-humans also experience and generate meaning about as they live. In this way, the hill becomes an important storied place, with each new generation, human and equine, learning from others who have inhabited this landscape. People notice and respond to changing weather and seasons in relation to their horses, and horses come to understand what to expect from the humans they share their lives with. This shared attention, practised over generations, is part of the very fabric of island life. Landscape is not a backdrop to this activity, it shapes and defines it – 'And loves it,' as I say aloud when I watch the ponies graze. Love is ever-present, in pony breeders' relationships not only with their ponies but with Shetland itself. I thought back to Tim Ingold's words that 'through living in it, the landscape becomes a part of us, just as we are a part of it'. Through living in this place, cultivating relationships with land and animals, embodying stories from the past while creating new connections into the future, pony breeders have truly become part of Shetland as Shetland has become part of them. As we live in this world, our thoughts, actions and intentions shape our interactions with those other than ourselves. We become who we are through our relationships with others – our soul, the essence of our being, created, and co-created, through these connections. Our attention to lives around us to human, animal, land, all matter. They make us who we are, the effects of these connections stretching through place and time, part of, yet also beyond, ourselves. As I sat on the hill, I felt certain that those who share our world feel and reciprocate this attention, that this ancient, wild and beautiful landscape loves those who live with it.

Stranded

The mist returned, swirling, opaque, pressing against the windows as we sat with packed bags, knowing if the weather did not change soon the flight home would be cancelled. Although the mist had begun to lift as we'd walked to our nearest neighbour's house, he confirmed that there would be no plane today. As this was not one of the ferry days, there was no way off the island. William invited us in for a cup of tea while he called Fran to check if we could stay another night. He reported back that it would be no problem, as it was not like any other visitor could arrive that day, and even if that was the case, 'nobody would see you stuck'. His words reassured me that we had a place to sleep, but I thought a little nervously about how low our supplies were getting. Since Foula had no shop, and weather strandings were always possible, I'd thought I had packed plenty spare in preparation, but we were now running alarmingly low on loo roll.

As he prepared the tea, I asked William if he had lived on Foula long. He replied, 'I grew up here, but have only been back to live here for a few years.' He paused. 'And now I know more about sheep than I ever meant to.' He laughed. 'They are all so different, you know – you start to tell them apart.' He'd once found an orphaned lamb on the hill. The lamb was weak and distressed so he'd brought him home and bottle-fed him until he was old enough to go out on the hill. He placed his hand over his eyes and said, 'Really he should be in the freezer – he's a useless sheep.' He was silent for a few moments before adding, 'He is really annoying. He has a very distinctive bleat. When I hear him outside I know it's him and then I need to go out and give him a few nuts.' I smiled, thinking of Yoda at home, and how falling in love with a caddy seemed inevitable. The care required to keep them alive in the early days involves close contact and attention, and these shared moments can create lasting connections. 'He is very friendly – maybe you saw him when you were out walking?' William asked, and I said that I had seen a large sheep with a fluffy golden fleece, that seemed tamer than the others. He nodded. 'That will be him, he has a lovely soft fleece.'

After we'd finished our tea and fruitcake and stood up to leave, William asked if there was anything we needed. I admitted our loo roll shortage and he went to get us some, along with some bread from the freezer and a little milk. As we stepped outside, William put some raisins from the cake on top of the wall, and they were immediately taken by a large blackbird, who seemed to have been waiting. 'Dipstick, I call him,' William said, gesturing to the departing bird. 'Always gets pushed around by the other birds but somehow he still raises a family every year.'

I smiled as walked back to our cottage. Despite William's seemingly harsh words about his caddy being useless, his attachment to the sheep was clear, as was his kindness, sharing his food with us as well as with the blackbird who lived in the garden wall. This combination of practical considerations and under-stated kindness was becoming familiar to me the more time I spent in Shetland. Crofters are not sentimental towards their animals. They respect them, but they also understand them as a resource: food for the freezer to sustain their family over a long winter, or a cheque following livestock sales. But this type of farming, with low numbers and close attention, is so different from more industrial farming: in Shetland's crofting relationships there is room for love.

I decided to spend the last day walking along the coastline. I could feel the sun behind the mist, infusing the cloud with warmth and light, but still much of the land remained invisible, shrouded. Fran and William had both said that predicting the path of the mist was next to impossible – sometimes with a little wind it could just shift, burned off by the sun; other times, with a gale that you would expect to clear it, it might stubbornly remain. My mind raced and I felt the familiar need to organise, micromanage, trying to plan for the unpredictable. I needed to get back to mainland Shetland. Supplies were running too low, and although I knew islanders would not leave us without, I didn't want to ask more from our neighbours, especially when it had been several days since the island had had supplies delivered. Even more pressing was that I had family coming to visit, arriving at 7am the following day from the overnight boat, who were expecting me to meet them. I had left a hasty voicemail, asking them to wait in Lerwick and I would be in touch once I knew what was happening. The Foula ferry was making a run to the mainland in the morning, and they had room for us, but it would arrive at Walls, about 30 miles from where we had parked our car at Tingwall airport. Or we could wait and see if the weather was suitable for the plane, which was due to leave an hour after the ferry – but if it didn't fly we would be stranded for at least one more night, possibly two dependent on the weather. I ran through the possibilities, over and over, feeling anxiety rise, before deciding that the boat was the only option, and trusting that we would find a way back to the car. I took a deep breath, trying to settle my mind, which seemed intent on second-guessing the decision by adding numerous 'what ifs' to the already unpredictable situation.

Through the mist I could hear, but not see, waves insistent against the rocks, their sound muffled, the shape of the Gadda stack occasionally visible, like sails of a spectral ship. What would the islanders think of me if they knew I was getting in such a fluster about travel arrangements? Their connection to the mainland is always uncertain, made possible or not through the ebb and flow of seasonal weather. People's lives are at the mercy of these forces as emergency access can be delayed or prevented altogether. I felt ashamed of my feelings. Just days after thinking I was becoming a less anxious person than I had been in the city, here I was, getting wound up over something relatively insignificant and over which I had little control.

I stopped walking, and breathed with the waves, letting my thoughts slow, my eyes tracing the intricacies of the stone I was sitting on. Sparse wiry grass emerged from the deeper crevices, although I could see no soil for their roots. Flat yellow lichen wove a pattern into the rough stone, while blue-grey tufts grew in patches. Although they each looked like one species, I knew that lichens are always two: a fungus and a partner photobiont. The photobiont transforms energy from the sun into food, a task the fungus is unable to do, and the fungus in turn provides an improved living environment. They live together, giving what the other needs in a complex symbiosis that we are yet to fully understand. Traces of wool, infused with water droplets from the air, attached to every surface. Geology, botany, farming, a tapestry, a world in stone.

I was learning how such attention to the landscape could calm me, how letting the feel of history and immediacy and the presence of life could transform my thoughts. These moments were enough to break my cyclical pattern of worries, so often self-perpetuating and consuming, far out of proportion to the events that started them. I realised that moving away from anxiety would be less of a transformation and more of a journey. I could feel a path away from it, but knew that to follow it would take practice.

5

PONIES IN JUMPERS

W E STOOD BY THE HORSEBOX, trying to dress Freckle in an overly large knitted jumper. She was understandably confused but was remarkably tolerant of the process. As Freckle tripped over her sleeves, which fully enveloped her hoofs, and the foal tried to chew at the unusual woollen garment, the ponies' owner, Amanda, and her mum, Marion, wondered aloud why an American travel show wanted to film Shetland ponies in Fair Isle jumpers.

The track gleamed white in the sun as it wound its way between green fields to the sandy beach below. We made an odd-looking procession, with two Fair Isle adorned ponies, a lively foal and two fluffy Shetland sheepdogs. A surprisingly large group followed us, carrying bags of equipment, drones, cameras, and long poles with fluffy microphones that the ponies seemed especially interested in. I stopped for a moment at the brow of the hill, startled by the sheer clarity of the light that made land and sea shine with a radiance so different from how I had known this place in winter. 'Won't need much of a filter,' I heard one of the crew say as he looked out to the turquoise sea, azure sky and golden sand.

The water rippled and there was a light whooshing sound as the breeze chased grains of sand. A family were having a picnic in the shelter of a sand dune, and at the sight of us the youngest child, also dressed in a Fair Isle jumper, squealed her excitement, with her mum urging her to 'go peerie ways' with the horses. After assurances from Amanda, the family approached, delightedly chatting to the horses and us and taking photos. Soon more people began crowding around, exclaiming at how cute they found the ponies, and asking if they usually wore jumpers. I could feel Amanda and Marion bristle as they answered politely but firmly that Shetland ponies were a strong hardy breed that did not even need to wear a winter rug. They were not usually dressed up in jumpers.

I sat with Marion as Amanda did an interview by the water's edge. She said that ever since a VisitScotland advert had used the image of Shetland ponies in jumpers, everyone seemed to want ponies dressed up like that. The camera crew suggested that the ponies, loose, running the length of the beach would make a good image for the programme. Amanda was hesitant, saying that this was not a place they were used to and so they would need to be given space. They looked beautifully majestic as they cantered along the expanse of sand. Then suddenly, a drone rose, buzzing loudly, flying low over their heads. Immediately the horses swerved, and galloped up the track, away from the beach. Amanda called out but they were gone. We ran up the path behind them, worried they might reach the main road. Once they had escaped the drone, however, they had stopped a short distance away, and were found contentedly grazing.

After this, it was decided to keep the mares on the halter but the foal could be free, as she would not stray far from her mum. Marion laughed and said the foal was getting a bit 'foo o' herself'' as she ran in tight circles, kicking up sand with her tiny hoofs and dart-ing a few steps into the water before making a hasty retreat. As the day wore on, and filming took longer than expected to complete, she slowed, reminding me of a toy running out of batteries, until she seemed almost asleep on her feet. When the camera crew left and the now-jumperless ponies were loaded into the horsebox, Amanda and Marion chatted anxiously, concerned that people watching the programme might think that Shetlanders really dressed their ponies up in woolly jumpers. They spoke about it being such a silly thing to do to a pony that is so strong and independent, questioning why people would want to film something so misrepresentative of the ponies and the place, worrying they might be 'making a mockery of us and our ponies'.

Island extinctions

That morning with the Fair Isle-adorned ponies started me thinking more about the power of representations. When we think about national and regional identities, we often consider how people see and describe themselves and other humans. If animals are connected to these identities, such as the British bulldog or the American bald eagle, they are considered symbols. Anthony P. Cohen, in his ethnography of Whalsay, describes symbols as vehicles through which communities represent and reiterate valued aspects of their culture. When Amanda and Marion had thought their ponies were being misrepresented they'd worried that 'us and our ponies' were being mocked, the representations of their horses extending to include the Shetland pony breed, the people who love and work with them, and Shetland itself. We often think of symbols as things that reveal a lot about people, but perhaps less about the animals being represented. However, across Shetland, island breeds are included as active participants in the stories of hard work and resourcefulness that are so central to local identities. Connections between animals, history and contemporary life are closely interwoven in ways that are powerfully symbolic, but the shared attributes between people and animals inform and are informed by everyday embodied relationships with the animals they love.

Pretty much everybody I spoke to drew contrasts between Shetland breeds and southern breeds, where the Shetland breeds exemplified the qualities of independence, intelligence and weather sense. In contrast, imported breeds such as Cheviot or Suffolk sheep have lost many of these qualities because of generations of domestication practices focused solely on increasing meat yield. But I soon learned that just because Shetland breeds had these qualities, it was not guaranteed that they always would. As they had been lost in other breeds, it was possible the same could happen here – that Shetland breeds could be at risk of becoming less 'Shetland'.

For some, there is a fear that these connections might have been lost in the case of the Shetland sheepdog. The 2003 *Shetland Times* book on Shetland breeds says of the sheepdog:

A consensus is clear: the dog called 'Shetland sheepdog' today is not the animal that arose in Shetland, thrived there until some time in the nineteenth century when it was replaced by mainland dogs, and yet survived well into the twentieth century. While the modern Shetland sheepdog may have distinct merits, it is not the indigenous animal that inhabited the island crofts, richly earned its keep and animated Shetland life for generations.

I only met a few Shetland sheepdogs and was surprised by how rarely they were mentioned in conversations about Shetland breeds. When I asked specifically, the answers varied, some saying they were never proper working animals, and others describing the breed's original purpose as one of herding sheep or staying close to the croft, barking to scare away animals that might damage the crops. Everybody agreed that they were now very different from how they would have been in the past. Although people occasionally identified attributes from today's breed as originating from their time as croft dogs, most believed contemporary Shetland sheepdogs were not a true native breed. Several people referred to them as a 'Victorian invention'. They are widely considered to be intelligent, but their tiny size and long coat means they are not thought of as a practical working animal and so not a 'true' Shetland breed.

I was still thinking about how the line is drawn

between true Shetland breeds and those who have lost their identity when I went to meet Agnes, who had been working with Shetland sheep for over eighty years. Despite it being mid-June, the rain was driving on a force 8 gale as Agnes and I walked down the road. Dressed head to toe in waterproofs, her back straight despite the wind, she turned to me and asked if I minded being out in this weather. Agnes said she had been going out to check sheep since she was four and 'a little wind doesn't bother Shetland people or Shetland sheep'. When she reached the fence she called 'Ka-ka-ka-ka-ka!' then turned to me and said, 'They'll be disappointed. Normally when I call them down like this I have food.'

The flock moved towards us, stopping a few feet from the fence, watching. As we talked the flock stood, grazing, occasionally looking up at us, but didn't come any closer or show any sign of demanding food or impatience that it was not given. Their thick fleeces were shades of grey, brown and white, and I noticed most of them had horns. 'The auld-type yowes all had horns,' Agnes explained. 'When the Shetland Flock Book Society was set up in 1927, this standardisation led to changes in the breed. These', she said, pointing to the sheep around us, 'are more authentic than the newer flock-book sheep. The auld type can find shelter anywhere – they know the weather and can find food even in the depth of winter. The newer type are still tough, but they have lost some of those instincts.' She described how one evening just before dusk, in the winter of 1947, she'd been confused to see her sheep standing in the full force of the gale, seemingly in the wrong place for the weather. In the night the wind changed direction, and the next morning the heaviest snow she had ever known covered the land. Had the sheep sheltered in the place that had seemed right the evening before, they would have been buried in deep drifts and perished. She said that all the old crofts would have had this hardy, old-type sheep, but over time, especially following the introduction of the flock book, the selection for softer fleece began to change the sheep. Although Shetland sheep are still independent compared with other breeds, they are becoming more reliant on humans for survival.

Agnes gestured to a distant hill where she kept sheep that didn't need any extra feed and could fend for themselves, except for routine checks and essential welfare. 'Flock-book sheep could never survive that way.' She pointed to a white yowe in the field, standing with its shoulders hunched: 'That one is cold, you can see from how she stands. And look at her fleece, the way it is parted down the middle – that can let the rain in. I won't breed from a sheep like that.'

Agnes has devoted much of her time to breeding

the old type of sheep and hopes to encourage people to value and preserve the unique abilities of Shetland sheep. 'You have to remember the stories – they tell you about the place, the people and animals. I keep telling the stories and I hope the younger ones listen.' Among those who work with Shetland breeds there is a concern about 'over-domestication', where through too much human interference the connections between breed and place are becoming lost, and with it, the ability of people to understand the land and animals they work with. These changes harm both humans and animals, separating them from the landscapes in which they thrive, and eroding the knowledge required to truly belong in Shetland.

Are Shetland ponies cute?

With their diminutive stature, thick, fluffy coat, and abundance of mane and tail, 'cute' is often the first word people associate with Shetland ponies. 'Awwwww, that is soooooooo cute!' was the usual response when I described my research project, and there were exclamations and cooing even within academic discussions at the university. At this time, an advert for the 3 mobile network featuring a moonwalking Shetland pony was being shared widely across social media, and dozens of people sent me the link commenting on the cuteness of the pony. Several times, early on, I joked that I might rename my thesis 'Dancing Pony Club: Ponies and Landscape in Shetland', without realising that the term 'cute' and associated practices could be considered harmful, potentially threatening the very future of the breed.

Something described as 'cute' will often have characteristics associated with infants: large eyes, endearing clumsiness, and a general air of juvenile dependence – the exact opposite of the strength and independence valued in Shetland breeds.

'Would you look at this!' Alice, a pony breeder, said to me as she showed me a video playing on her phone. Two Shetland ponies, one dressed in a top hat and the other wearing a bridal veil, were getting married. Although the idea that some folk found ponies cute was becoming familiar to me, I had never seen anything like this. 'Pet breeders,' she said, shaking her head. 'They're ruining the breed with this sort of nonsense.' 'Pet breeders' was a term I had heard often from people in Shetland, referring to a particular type of breeder, usually from the south of England, who would have a small number of 'cute' ponies that they would anthropomorphise and overly domesticate, practices seen as the very opposite of the responsible pony breeders in Shetland.

Many breeders told me about how pet breeders

would, with little knowledge about horses, buy a cute Shetland pony and then keep it in a tiny field by their house or even in their garden. They would then decide their pony should have a husband and so would buy a colt, usually at a low price from a sale. Keeping a mare and a stallion together in this way would usually result in the arrival of a foal.

In some cases, pet breeders keep the foals they breed, to have the foal live with their mother and father. Breeders in Shetland were openly contemptuous of such practices. Ponies were being treated like human children, encouraged to live with their parents as a nuclear family. Having ponies 'marry' and live in this way is based on anthropomorphic projection rather than any desire to understand the true needs and wishes of the animals. By refusing to acknowledge ponies' identities as equines, while simultaneously underestimating their intelligence and capacity to have their own opinions, pet breeders were thought to be acting in a very harmful way. Although, unlike many other UK native breeds, Shetland ponies are not deemed 'at risk', due to low numbers there are concerns that ponies could change into something that bears little resemblance to the ponies that have been such an important part of Shetland's lives and landscapes. Practices to breed ever-smaller animals and treat them like cute toys, overly domesticating them by controlling too much of their lives and not giving them the freedom and space to have their own opinions, is thought, over time, to change the behaviour of ponies and the ways that people relate to the breed. Breeders in Shetland passionately believe that, even though their ponies are small, it is vital to remember that they are horses and ensure we treat them as such. Restricted living areas or unnatural herd dynamics were thought to be deeply upsetting for the animals, resulting in negative behaviours, which affect the reputation of the breed.

As the breed's reputation changes, thought of as either a cute toy or a disagreeable 'Shitland', people may overlook the skills that make the breed a good rising pony, a trusted companion or a capable work-horse. Shetland breeders are not simply worried that the breed they love is changing – Shetland ponies have always been adaptable, but this threat is different as it could disrupt connections, formed over generations, between ponies, people and place. The breed exists as part of a complex network of relationships, through which people and animals create, and are created by, island life. If we treat ponies in a way that causes their bodies and minds to forget how they were shaped by the wild hill, the Shetland wind, the loving care of crofters, then they lose something very special.

June explained it to me: 'Because o' domestication, da wye dat a lot o' dem is kept you canna tell whether they're stupid or intelligent because dae dinna hiv da opportunities to show you. Things lik da wadder an' predictin' da wadder an' bein' able ta find your ain shelter an' dat kinda things – if you ir staandin' in a peerie paddock wi post an' rail fencin' an' a stable, you dinna hiv da need tae do dat, an' dat instinct must leave you ... An' dan if you hae foals you dinna hae dat knowledge ta pass ontae dem.'

Incorrect or inconsiderate domestication practices could, in just a few generations, change connections between pony and place, destroying centuries of intergenerational knowledge. This loss would affect how Shetland is experienced by folk who live there: those who see the hill herds and remember their grandparents' stories, those who feel joy at the new foals in spring, and people whose everyday experience of land and weather is felt in relation to their ponies. For people and ponies to live together, to belong, both partners have a role to play. The ponies learn from each other, their owners and the land: memory of place, embodied in their genes and taught by those they live with. The attention pony breeders pay, to story and history, allows them to learn and respond to the land and animals, ensuring the continuation of these relationships into the future.

Spring to summer

Until I lived in Shetland, I hadn't realised how much the journeys of trees – from bare branches, to bud, then leaf, transforming from delicate green to fiery vibrancy – affected my perception of season. Now, with no trees to tell this story, I felt myself drawn to the subtler signs of change: the colours of the ground, songs of birds, the feel of the light. The change of seasons was slow, almost imperceptible, but one morning, it was suddenly summer. The sun was high in the sky, the clarity of light intensifying the colours of this landscape of hill, sea, flowers and sheep. A mirror sea reflected worlds of rock, cloud and dancing fulmar, while turnstone and sanderling darted in and out of gently lapping waves. Seaweed along the ebb crackled and popped as the tide retreated. In the distance an otter hunted, each descent beneath the surface leaving rings of silver, stretching further and further before being absorbed by the gentle rhythm of the water. The lichen grew with renewed vigour, blue-grey, green, yellow, now accompanied by sea pinks, stretching tall from patches of green that appeared to grow straight from bare rock. From the hill, the sheep watched but made no move towards me, the newly growing grass more enticing than the sheep nuts I might carry.

Amidst the sounds of lark and curlew, I heard a sudden, loud exhale of breath. Startled, I looked around and saw nobody near that could have made such a sound. Then again, a snort this time, followed by a splash. From the sea, dolphins rose, exhaled, then slipped below the surface. There must have been thirty or more, the waves they created the only movement in the still sea. I soon learned that these were not in fact dolphins but porpoises, neesicks in Shetland dialect. The sound when they surface is so distinct that if someone is a little out of breath it is said they are 'panting like a neesick'.

Flowers had emerged from seemingly barren ground, filling the garden with colour. I had continued to work, planting, weeding, enjoying the smell of earth and the feeling of touching life. When the large patch at the bottom of the garden was clear I had planted potatoes and carrots, following Robbie's advice on what varieties would grow best. But as winter had become spring and spring moved towards summer, rain continued to fall. Days of low cloud and constant drizzle, and bright days where the wind brought unexpected torrential downpours; we had more rain than anybody could remember. This unusual weather filled conversations, with pony breeders, in the shops, and on the ferry as water filled my newly planted garden.

The earth was saturated, and a large puddle in the

field beside the garden grew to such a size that it temporarily became home to two swans. I watched raindrops dance and splash on the water above where the potatoes were planted and knew they wouldn't grow unless I cleared it, so I started to dig two large ditches from the vegetable patch to the field beyond. It was exhausting work, the wet earth difficult to dig and heavy to carry, but when I was finished, water flowed out and the puddles reduced. Feeling how wet the earth was, I dug up a young potato to see if they were surviving, and to my horror found it had disintegrated into smelly green sludge. The whole crop was ruined. Robbie assured me there was still time to plant more and they should grow fine if I could keep the area dry, so with determined enthusiasm I dug the ditches deeper, turned the soil to help it dry, added compost and raised the beds, and planted a new crop of potatoes and carrots.

The kale and cauliflower seedlings in the porch still appeared small and spindly, unlikely to survive even a light breeze any time soon, so I bought some cauliflower plants that were past the awkward seedling stage and were ready to plant out. As I added them to the vegetable patch and planted some poppies (whose packet guaranteed their hardy nature), Lowrie came over to see how I was doing. He reassured me that the weather was making things difficult even for experienced gardeners, but he wondered if the drainage of the area might have changed since Margaret and Willie had grown vegetables, with more of the water from the hill ending up in the garden. I asked if there was anything I could do. He shook his head and said to just keep trying to dig drainage, and hopefully the weather would dry out soon. 'Next year, you can dig a patch up where I grow my veg – there is plenty space I don't use,' he offered.

He opened the boot of his car to reveal boxes of seed potatoes. 'Look,' he said, as he got a knife and sliced a small amount off a small, dark, knobbly potato. Inside was a beautiful purple marbling. 'This is the auld Shetland type, the Shetland black.' He explained that once this would have been the potato that everybody on the islands grew, but over time other types became prevalent and the native potato risked dying out. 'There are still lots dey ca' Shetland black, and on the outside they look the sam' but inside they dinna hiv this pattern – that's how you tell the difference.' He handed me one from the box and said to try it in my garden. I was grateful, but terrified that my ineptitude might kill a member of an endangered breed. As Lowrie left, he said two of his geese had laid eggs for the first time since he'd got them. 'I thought they were far too auld, but it shows you niver can tell!' He smiled. In the sun, as I planted the Shetland potato in the driest patch, close to where garden flowers met wildflowers by the boundary fence, listening to the sounds of sea, swans and larks, I felt a renewed optimism towards my garden.

Hirta

Towards the end of June, as I walked with Yoda on the ness, I felt hopeful as he had been showing more interest in the sheep and they were appearing less wary of him. He trotted behind me as I approached the flock. Four White Feet moved closer, followed by two other yowes, one with a grey-and-white fleece and pink nose, the other completely black apart from a white V marking across her face. They stood back as Four White Feet sniffed at Yoda and then nuzzled his face. He stood still and then started to rub his head against hers and then start to sniff underneath her, looking for milk. Objecting to this, Four White Feet darted away, back to the flock and stood watching us. Bleating loudly, Yoda ran towards the flock. Starey Sheep stepped forward, put his head down, and butted Yoda, hard. Yoda ran back to me, hiding behind me, still bleating. Moments later he ran towards the flock again, straight towards Starey Sheep, who again butted him until he ran away. I led an angry, bellowing Yoda back to the garden, gave him his bottle, and watched as he bounced around, seemingly unaffected by the unfortunate sheep encounter.

When I returned from my walk I got a phone call from a livestock officer. When I'd got Yoda, his owner had given me paperwork to fill in, detailing where he had lived and where he was now living. These documents are a legal requirement for tracing livestock in the event of disease outbreaks. I had filled in all my information – name, address etc. – but had left the space for holding number blank as I do not have a croft. The woman on the phone told me that the details were incomplete, and when I told her I didn't have a croft she asked me to explain exactly where the sheep was being kept. Although I had Lowrie's permission for Yoda to be on his land, I didn't know if this was official, or if by saying he was on his land if I might get Lowrie in trouble. I answered vaguely, saying he was a caddy and lived in the garden. She explained that this was not good enough and that I would need to provide correct information or my actions would be in breach of the law. As soon as I hung up, I started to panic. Lowrie had been so kind to give a home to the caddy I'd brought home, an action that I had not thought through, and I didn't want to cause him any more trouble. If I couldn't give his holding number then what would I do? And what would happen to Yoda?

The next morning, I nervously waited for the sound of Lowrie's quad bike, just like I had on Yoda's first day. Immediately, he reassured me that there was no issue with Yoda being on the land, and there was just a lot of paperwork with sheep. Even so, he was surprised that there was so much fuss over a caddy, which would never be a breeding animal and would not be moving again. 'Jist doin' their job I guess.' He shrugged. 'Call them back with my holding number – won't cause any problems. He has his tags and is counted among my flock.' Relieved, I thanked him, feeling terrible to have imposed, once again, on his kindness.

When I got off the phone with the animal movement department, who seemed appeased by my giving them a holding number, I got a text from Roselyn saying she was just going to do some work with Hirta, who was now in her care, if I would like to come along? As I walked along the road to meet her, the sky was heavy with cloud and the wind held a hint of rain. The steel-grey sea carried fast-moving white horses, their bright bodies lit by invisible sun. A brown-and-white stallion pranced by the water's edge, lifting his feet high, tossing his head as his mane moved with the wind.

Roselyn pointed out the house she'd grown up in, and several other houses where her family still lived, as we walked up to the field. When I asked if her father working with ponies had influenced her love of horses, she said it was a bit different. Her dad hadn't thought of them as Shetland ponies like we do now: 'For him, she was Jean the horse, his friend who he loved, and who helped him bring home the peat every year.' She laughed at how, as a child, he would 'skive off school to bring in the peat fae the hill'. She paused. 'But I am certain horses are in my blood. Always have been. I begged and begged and got a Shetland pony when I was thirteen.' She had not previously known much about the breed, but when she got this pony she loved her so much she wanted to know everything about her. She'd had a slip of paper detailing her pedigree and where she was in the stud-book, 'And I started to learn about the breed and its history. Folk working with the Shetland Pony Stud-Book Society could see my interest and invited me to be involved.'

'She is here to find herself,' Roselyn said, repeating the phrase June had used when describing Hirta's move to Whalsay. She fastened the mare's halter and led her to the gate, where she tied her up, before retrieving brushes from a shed overflowing with tack, grooming kits, riding hats and myriad other horse-related items. As we brushed Hirta's sleek coat, Roselyn said that today we would just be doing a little work to get her started, and that her thirteen-year-old daughter Rebecca would be doing most of the work over the summer. Rebecca was away that week to compete in the Shetland Pony Grand National on mainland Scotland, and would start working with Hirta as soon as she returned.

Hirta stood quietly, ears twitching as I groomed her, and Roselyn began to place the bridle over her head, gently putting the bit in her mouth and fastening the buckles. She chewed at the bit, rolling it between teeth and tongue. 'I think this is the first time she has had a bridle on,' Roselyn said, scratching the mare's neck. When I mentioned how calm Hirta seemed she replied, 'You can tell June has worked wi her a lot. It makes a big difference when folk spend time with ponies like that. Means they are happy to be worked with. Look,' she said as she ran her hands along Hirta's flanks and underneath where a girth would go. Hirta stood calmly, not objecting to this touch. 'You can tell she has been touched like this before. Makes it a lot easier when it is time to put a saddle on.'

Roselyn took a girth with a pad on it and started to fasten it around Hirta's middle, explaining that it is best to start with something light. It allows them to get used to the sensation of the girth without the weight of a saddle. We led her down to the road. Hirta walked confidently, ears pricked forward; when a car passed she watched with interest. 'Looks like June has had her oot on the road before.' Roselyn smiled. We went along the road, alternating between walking and trotting, until Roselyn decided that that was enough for the day – she didn't want to push her too hard on her first time. As Hirta trotted up the hill, back to her herd, Roselyn said she was delighted with how well Hirta had done, and she thought that she had the makings of 'a very fine riding horse'.

I asked if that meant she had 'found herself'. Roselyn laughed and said she thought she had but time would tell. She explained that Shetland ponies love to be useful, but what that means for each pony can be different – that was why they were giving Hirta a chance to try new things. 'Take the likes o' Idiot: he was born to race. As soon as his tack is on he gets so excited he bounces, runs his race, and wants to do more, loves every minute. Yitter on the other hand . . . Good horse, great wi bairns and leadrope, but would never want to race like Idiot. You have to learn what each one enjoys, follow their lead, and it looks like Hirta will love being a riding pony.'

I asked Roselyn why being useful was so important for Shetland ponies. She said that Shetland ponies 'love tae do a job o' work. They were always a workhorse and they thrive when they hae a chance to be useful.' She worried that they were no longer seen as useful animals and so it was essential to 'get the message out that they are not this dumpy, peerie dope on a rope. They are as intelligent, if not more intelligent, as any other equine. You shouldn't dismiss them because they are peerie.' She said that if that gets forgotten, and people breed without appropriate knowledge, then the future of the Shetland pony breed is at risk. 'This is why it is so important to have good Shetland ponies in Shetland – this is where they came from, why they ir the way they ir. We ir, and need to remain, the centre of the Shetland pony universe.' She asked if I was going to the stallion assessments due to take place the following week, and when I said I was she said, 'These assessments are so important. Shetland is the only place in Britain that assesses stallions in this way now.' After an EU ruling that prevented the mandatory assessment of stallions prior to breeding, many in Shetland feared that ponies of inferior quality were now being allowed to breed, passing on unwanted characteristics and threatening the future of the breed. The Pony Breeders of Shetland Association developed a voluntary assessment, where people could have their stallions evaluated by three judges and be awarded gold, silver or bronze. Roselyn said, 'Lots o' ponies in the assessments this year, an' it's in Unst too. Hopefully more an' more people will enter: it'll really help maintain the quality of island-bred ponies.'

Stallion assessment

As my alarm sounded at 5.30am, I could see golden light spilling through the curtains. I tried to rouse myself to be on time for the 6.30 ferry and the journey to Unst, but as waves of exhaustion flowed over my body, I lay back down and fell asleep. Waking in a panic some hours later, I rushed into the car, and drove to Symbister, hoping there would be space in the standby queue for the next ferry to the mainland. It was the day of the Whalsay Gala and Symbister was the busiest I had ever seen it. Women and children flowed into the public hall; outside a hand-painted sign promised FACE PAINTING, HOOK-A-DUCK, and GUESS THE MINION'S BIRTHDAY. By the marina groups of men, dressed in flat caps and Fair Isle ganseys, stood by tiny boats, more of which sailed in the sheltered bay for a miniature boat race.

Three ferry journeys later, I arrived in Unst and drove north to the furthest tip of the island, Herma-ness. The ocean stretched vast before me, the island of Muckle Flugga the only land visible. Beyond that lies Greenland, Svalbard and the North Pole. Local legend says the island formed when giants Herma and Saxa both fell in love with a mermaid and fought each other for her affection by throwing huge rocks, one of which became Muckle Flugga. For a time the light-house, perched precariously on top of this tiny island, was the most northerly inhabited part of Britain, until automation in 1955 saw the last lighthouse keeper leave. Even on this relatively still day, waves splashed at the foot of the cliffs, and I tried to imagine how it would have felt to live there during Shetland's wild winter months. I later learned that in rough weather, crew were winched from boats to the lighthouse, suspended on ropes above the crashing waves.

I followed a long wooden boardwalk that wound its way over rugged peatland. Around me the bog cotton was beginning to fade, fluff separating from stalks, strewn; those caught on heather potentially next year's plants, others blown out to sea, lost. The rough, wiry heather appeared softer, dressed in summer green. In the spaces between, delicate pink and yellow flowers grew next to extravagant orchids. Towards land's edges, there was thrift in abundance. I walked amidst a seaside flower meadow in summer, but the scent of the wind carried something far less floral than the surroundings might suggest. Nauseating, overpowering, like ammonia and fish, the unmistakable stench of guano hinting at what lay further along this track.

As I walked, I encountered bonxies, perched on top of tussocks, watchful. Some swooped above, but no divebombings; they must be used to sharing this place with people on the path. I was surprised to see how big the chicks were – it had only been a few weeks since I'd seen that comically long-legged fluffball on Foula. These babies now resembled the parent birds, their wings already adorned with some flight feathers, their beaks large and sharp. They followed their parents, hunch-backed, emitting continual peevish whines, reminding me of urban seagulls in both sound and movement.

Where the land stopped, cloud-marbled sky reflected its pattern onto the sea, and the world of birds truly began. Guano-coated rocks and stacks glowed bright in the sun, and the wind carried the clamouring cries of millions of voices. The squawks of guillemot and razorbill rose from ledges just above white-crested waves, fulmar croaked and cawed from below the thrift, while distant calls of kittiwakes echoed around the cliffs. However, it was the gannets that took my breath away. Towering cliffs, weathered into hundreds of ledges, with each available crevice inhabited by gannet pairs. Through binoculars I could see the details of their pale yellow heads: black lines crossed their razor-sharp beaks, and I was struck by their unblinking blue eyes. They seemed so close I felt I was intruding on their homes, a voyeur. On powerful wings, hundreds more filled the sky, as they journeyed out to sea in search of food, or returned to their nests with fish for their partner and chicks.

As the sun began to lower towards the horizon, I drove to my hotel, stopping at the Lund Stone. Standing alone, this stone has watched over this place for

5,000 years, witness to Norse settlements and ancient churches, to changing lives and landscapes. Feeling drawn to it, I reached out, touching its rough surface, the living moss coating this stone of stories. As curlew called, I looked from stone to sky, and spoke my hopes and dreams, my greatest wish. I felt the air shift, a gust of wind, powerful, intimate, part of day and night, land and sea, and I felt heard, acknowledged. The next day, my wish came true.

The next morning, under a cloud-laden sky that kept threatening rain, I watched ponies walking and trotting round the ring and tried to concentrate, but I was distracted, unable to fully follow conversations or keep up with my notes. I kept going to the toilet, partly as I seemed constantly desperate to pee, but also to check: was I bleeding? I was not, despite my period being due days before. My heart soared. I had felt like this might be the month I was pregnant, noticing subtle signs of change, but knowing how my imagination could get the better of me, I needed to take a test before I could allow myself to believe. I arrived home at dusk after the second day of assessments and immediately went to the bathroom. I watched the egg timer symbol on the test, nervous, but at the same time I *knew* what it would say. PREGNANT 1–2 WEEKS.

Back home, over the next few days, as I walked, my thoughts and feelings felt like they were overflowing, that there was more than could be contained within my body. At the centre of it all, I felt a strong sense of peace and happiness that this path to motherhood was the one I should be walking. The time was right and I was ready. Yet doubts niggled, about what I had to offer. I thought of the families I saw around me, networks of relationships, aunts, uncles, cousins, grandparents, connections to land, animals and history. Roots. Something I didn't have to give. I thought back to my own childhood. Both my parents were only children, my mum's parents had died before I was born, and I'd lost my grandfather at four and my grandmother at fourteen. My parents rarely had friends visiting, and when I thought of the sounds of childhood homes, the only voices I remembered were those of my parents or Radio 4. Events associated with families, like Christmas, were celebrated with just me and my parents until their divorce when I was nine, after which it would be Christmas dinner with Mum and then a visit to Dad's house.

I grew up rurally: my friends were the chickens, goat and donkey, the flowers, insects and my imagination. My first day of school was a shock. With no experience of siblings or children my own age, I just didn't know what to do. Lessons were OK, with structure, activities and a kind teacher, but I dreaded breaktime. Shrinking back against the playground wall, I watched, not understanding the games and chatter, longing to join in but not knowing how. In the morning, I would wait by the school gate for the teacher to arrive, so I had someone to talk to. I tended a tiny oak seedling by the playground wall, dreaming of the day it would become a tree, fantasising about climbing high in its branches, escaping from that place of concrete and confusion.

Thinking of this in relation to a new life growing inside me changed my feelings about the past, intensifying the loneliness that I realised I still felt. I was adrift, always a little lost. When it was time to announce the pregnancy, share our joy, it would be over the phone to far-away family members. There was no easy solution – with mine and Steve's families dispersed across the country, not tied to the places they inhabited, there was no possibility of us returning 'home' to start our family. Whatever belonging is, it was something I'd always had to work to find. Now, I wondered, would I be able to give a sense of security and home to my own child? Thinking of how people understood Shetland to be in their blood, a deep sense of home and belonging connecting them to the islands they love, I wondered if impermanence might be in my own blood. With no place attached to my family and a passion for change and exploration, I had moved house many times, the journey to Shetland just one of many new places. Even now, as I longed for a sense of home, I found it difficult to imagine being in one place for ever. Although it felt tempting and something I wished for, I simultaneously turned away from the idea, finding it limiting, claustrophobic. Did that mean contradiction was in my blood? And if I couldn't figure out what I wanted from life, what would this mean for my child?

One day, as I stood watching the sea, a movement caught my eye: a long, curved back with a small fin emerged, then slipped below the waves in one fluid movement. Minutes later, a little distance away, I saw it again. In the sea, a minke whale travelled alongside me, alongside us. In the same moment, a rainbow materialised, forming a bridge between land and sea, earth and sky. A reminder that connection to place can emerge from these moments, opportunities and encounters to build on. A realisation that roots needn't depend on specific histories – there are many ways to grow. In that moment, I felt a sense of calm returning. There was so much beauty in the world to share with my child. We may not have a home as such, but together, as a family, we would create one. Making home through a shared journey of love.

6

SHOW PREPARATION

THE ALARM SOUNDED, HIGH-PITCHED and insistent. Silencing it, I lay back down and closed my eyes. Waves of nausea flowed through me, their intensity such that it felt as if my body, the bed, the whole world, were moving. I lay still, hoping it would pass. Of course, I had heard of morning sickness, friends describing difficult times in their own pregnancies, but I had not expected this. A clawing sickness, a feeling of whole-body weakness, and an aversion to almost all foods didn't just characterise the mornings, but accompanied me all day. I was entering one of the busiest times in my fieldwork: the lead-up to the summer livestock shows. I needed to be active, present and attentive, and yet it felt like I was fighting against my own body. 'Baby,' I said, 'I love you but can you please make me a little less sick? Just a little?'

The ferry crossing was rough, as a brisk wind from

the east drove the waves sideways, causing the boat to judder and lurch. I sat in the lounge, where the windows gave me a horizon to focus on. I watched the land passing slowly while I half listened to a father tell his children a story about the hardy sheep who live by themselves on an island nearby. I caught sight of my reflection. I appeared pale and drawn – that I had expected, but I was surprised to see the lines of worry etched across my face. Since discovering I was pregnant, I was noticing every bodily change and twinge, wondering if they were normal or if they could indicate a problem. I had googled miscarriage, hoping to put my mind at rest slightly, only to discover with horror that one in four pregnancies end this way. I couldn't get it out of my mind, even phoning the maternity department, seeking reassurances that nobody could give. My sickness provided some comfort, seeming to confirm I was indeed pregnant, and there had been no reduction in my symptoms. Yet the sickness also brought a certain unease: I felt just too unwell to believe that me and my baby could be healthy. Signs of anxiety began to surface: repeatedly taking pregnancy tests to be sure the line was getting darker; analysing my symptoms in relation to the Ready Steady Baby! app, and spending far too much time and attention reading threads on pregnancy message boards, as if the outcome of strangers' pregnancies had any bearing on my own.

The worst was not being able to tell anybody how I felt. I feared that breaking the 'twelve-week rule' would be tempting fate, and so I tried to carry on as normal, hiding my sickness and worry as best I could.

As I drove along the winding roads of the west mainland, I began to relax, my attention drawn to the world around me, away from my worries. The heather-coated hills were beginning to take on the purple sheen from which blossoms would soon emerge. Once-tiny lambs now roamed further from their mothers, joining peers in explorations of the hill, the sound of their voices joining the song of curlew as they kept a constant communication with the flock.

I approached Jackie's croft, a small white stone house surrounded by sea and hill, the presence of Foula, silhouetted on the horizon, adding to the magic of the scene. Jackie had moved to Shetland twenty years previously. Soon after her arrival she had gone to the Lerwick pony sale, where she'd fallen in love with a filly She'd told herself that if she could get the pony for the same price she had got selling a pair of riding boots, then she would buy her. She had expected the price to go far higher, but to her surprise, hers was the winning bid, and from that day on she had kept and bred ponies. Her croft was always a hive of activity. In addition to the horses, she kept sheep, cattle, hens and turkeys. Each individual was known, their quirks expected and accepted. Jackie was one of the first pony breeders I had met, and on learning that I wanted to get experience with horses she had suggested I could help show her ponies that summer.

I could see Jackie outside, her three Jack Russells dancing excitedly around her. After she had bundled the reluctant dogs inside, promising them more walks later, she turned to me. 'Right, let's get some horses caught and I'll teach you how to show them.' We walked through the yard where free-range hens and turkeys roamed, dodging the advances of an adult caddy who had decided to return to the croft for a visit. 'Need to get her back up to the hill,' Jackie said, as the sheep bleated with excitement and tried to follow us, only turning away and darting back to the yard as we opened the gate to her field. Mares and foals grazed where previous crofthouses had stood, their crumbling walls providing shelter for new generations, while the sound of lark and curlew filled the sky, seeming to come from all directions at once, neither close nor far, just present.

We led several mares down to the yard. Tawney, a leggy two-year-old, bright chestnut with a blaze; Midnight, a quiet blue roan, and Ellen, a petite, pretty bay. Taking them to the gate, Jackie said that these were the ponies I would be working most closely with, and that I should take the time to get to know them, visiting whenever I could to practise with them. As we worked, she showed me how to get them to stand so that their weight was evenly distributed, as a poor standing position could give the impression of incorrect proportions. She taught me how to use differing pressure on the rope to encourage a flowing gait, to demonstrate the pony's good movement.

Another day, Bjørn joined us to share some of his show experience. He emphasised the importance of paying attention to the pony. They must always be in the best position, standing well and looking interested, as the judge could look your way at any moment. He emphasised that no pony was perfect, even the very good ones, and one of the arts of showing was to draw attention to the pony's strongest features and distract from their poorer ones. He turned to Midnight, and said she was a good strong horse but her head was a little plain. Taking the rope, he moved with her, encouraging her to flex her neck, and as she stood, with sunlight on her dappled coat, she did appear even more beautiful.

I visited throughout the spring and summer, as the marsh marigold gave way to wild iris and orchids bloomed across the landscape. Slowly, I learned how to move with the ponies, understanding the feel on the rope, interpreting their mood. But although my confidence grew as the weeks past, I was increasingly aware of my pregnant body. A feeling of weakness where I would expect to be strong, and an unexpected fear.

Whenever the horse I was working with spooked or pulled hard against the rope, I worried about accidents, falls or kicks to my stomach. One time, Midnight pulled so hard that I felt myself moving, falling forward. I let go of the rope, allowing her to run away, something I'd been taught never to do. But I had been too worried that an injury to me could hurt the baby. With this anxiety came another fear: Jackie had opened up her home to me, shared her stories about life with her animals, and had taken the time to patiently teach me how to show her horses. Due to mobility problems she was not able to show her ponies herself, and I needed to do a good job at the shows, or I knew I would be letting her down.

Breed and shows

All my visits to pony breeders that summer were filled with talk of shows. With fewer opportunities to show ponies in Shetland than there would be on the mainland, the summer agricultural shows were particularly important. The pony classes had sections for different ages and sexes of pony, where each horse entered was assessed by a professional judge according to the breed standard. Breeders explained the importance of show success. Adding awards next to ponies' names on stud websites or sales catalogues could affect prices and influence the reputation of the stud. But it was more than just economic; there was a real sense of pride and achievement when the hard work of breeding, the time, care and attention, was recognised and rewarded. Although across Shetland there was a strong desire to breed ponies with characteristics associated with horses from the island's past, what that meant to each stud, in practice, varied. People wanted to breed ponies of a particular type, that could be recognised as part of their stud.

June explained: 'My idea of breeding is, I ken whit I lik. I ken whit my goals are. They are not big goals but I ken whit they are, an' that's to produce a big, heavy, solid, good-movin' pony wi nice temperament, an' if I can git them black an' white then I'm happy. I lik me colours. An' that's whit I'm wantin', I'm no wantin' to win big fancy shows an' that; I just want to look out an' be happy at whit I see. I think that you should create your own type, your own breed, you ken. That folk can look an' say, "Yun must hae sumthin' to do wi June." Now, I can do that. I do it among my ain ponies, but I can also look at a lot o' ponies in a ring and say, "I bet that one goes back to Spangle o'Berry," you ken. They hae a type aboot them. I mind a few year ago, Edwin, a retired vet – I mind him coming to the evaluations a few year ago, and I didn't hae this stallion there, but he said, "Oh, yun must hae sumthin to do wi de," an' I said, "Yeah, my old guy's his grandfather," an' he said, "Yeah, yeah, I thought dat." Now that, to me – I was just buzzin'. I couldna care if I had gotten fuck-all at the evaluations. That was enough for me, 'cos somebody could pick out my type o' pony among the rest.'

June's joy came from her breeding being apparent in the body of a pony. He was known and recognised as one of hers. She showed me a folder where she had recorded her studs' genealogies. Although many studs are part of this family tree, ponies connected to the Wells or Berry studs are highlighted, and lines of red and blue weaved their way through the diagram. As we talked, she would often point to a name on the paper, telling stories of each horse: how she fell in love with her stallion Urban of Knowe, the relationship they had developed over the years, the foals he had produced. Toni, the matriarch and teacher. Belle O' Berry, long dead but still present through her influence, her characteristics still apparent in ponies born to the stud today. Watching ponies, learning the attributes associated with particular lines, and understanding how these work in practice were key to June's breeding. She didn't want either the Berry or Wells line to come through too strong, she hoped to combine the characteristics she liked, adapting and improvising with experience, learning through love.

When I first met Carole from the Gue stud she showed me a trophy she had won at the Unst Show. Her fingers traced the metal, across the names of previous winners, stopping when she reached another Gue pony that her father had owned many years ago. Carole described how winning in Unst, where the Gue stud originated, had been particularly meaningful, as she'd felt it connected her daily practice to the stud's history. The ponies she'd inherited were mostly grey in colour and mid-size height. Over the years she had introduced more colours and had reduced size, by breeding with the smaller ponies and choosing minis when she bought ponies. Not wanting a reduction in size to be accompanied by a loss of bone, she carefully chose ponies with the height and build she liked, and where possible chose ponies whose lines contained some of the old Gue bloodlines. As we stood, looking out across her fields at the beautiful mix of chestnut, grey and roan ponies, Carole explained that pony breeding was something that had to be done for love, not money. She said it was love, for ponies and for the family tradition of breeding, that had led her to take on the stud following her uncle's death. And although Carole took great pride in the connection between her practice and that of the breeders before her, it was blending this continuity with innovation, shaping the line to create her type, that brought her the most joy.

Size, colour, bone and movement were attributes regularly mentioned by breeders, as they emphasised the importance of carefully planning which mares and stallions to combine each year. Although there was never a guaranteed result from a particular union, a degree of knowledge and foresight was hoped to ensure the resulting offspring would be good ponies whose characteristics adhered to the breed standard. It was not enough to know an individual pony; a responsible breeder was expected to know their ponies' bloodlines. A central part of breeding practice, then, was understanding what had come before, knowing what you wanted to produce, and making decisions on this basis.

Noticing

Now that Yoda was older he lived full-time in the sheep field – he was now too big to squeeze out the gaps. I had reduced his bottles and had introduced hard feed into his diet. Sheep nuts promised to provide all the nutrition that a growing lamb might need, and Yoda loved them. On hearing the sound of the bag he would bound over, kicking his heels in the air. Unfortunately, if I threw the nuts over the fence to him, Yoda was somehow unable to find them in the grass. He would look around for a moment, before staring at me, bleating insistently, sometimes using his hoofs to paw noisily at the gate. So I started putting his nuts in a small bowl . The other sheep were quick to learn that most of Yoda's lunch could be theirs. At the sound of his feeding time, they would circle him, a continually moving woolly mass, waiting for the nuts that fell out the bowl and were lost to Yoda. Sometimes, if they thought I was gone, some would approach Yoda, butting him, or gently but insistently moving him away from his bowl. He never objected to this, he just stood back looking so sad that I couldn't bear it. I started scattering some nuts for the other sheep whenever I filled Yoda's bowl, so they would leave him in peace to eat. After they had finished, the flock would walk in a line up the hill, but two sheep, Four White Feet and a black sheep with a white moustache, would wait behind. They'd stand with Yoda and nuzzle him, before moving a few steps away towards the other sheep. When he didn't follow, they would stop several times, *baa*-ing at him, encouraging him to come with them. They did this every day, seeming not to lose patience. Sometimes, for a moment, it looked like Yoda might understand, when he walked a few steps as if to follow them, before returning to stand alone at the gate.

I began noticing the starlings, how they would perch along the walls of the old crofthouse, their song building and changing as more joined the group. They were always there, waiting, before I fed Yoda. I didn't feed him at the same times – there was no predictable routine – and yet there they always were. I started to pay attention, noticing how I could walk to Yoda's field, or into the garage where the feed was kept, and be completely ignored, and yet if I was planning to feed him the starlings knew. I realised that something of my intention was visible to them, they could sense a change in my movement, a shift in my focus, as they read the changing rhythms of the landscape.

One still morning, Robbie pointed out to sea where gulls were calling and diving into the shallows. 'That means there are piltocks close to shore.' He described how, when they were children, he and his friends would all go out onto the rocks with their fishing rods whenever they saw the birds moving in this way. Easy to catch in the right conditions, piltocks were a valuable resource, as, salted and dried, they could be stored for times of shortage. Robbie said most folk now would go out to sea for mackerel or lobster, but you could still occasionally see piltocks hung to dry on island washing lines. I watched the gulls, seeing the dimpling of the water surface that indicated fish moving just below the surface.

I loved these moments, when with attention, the everyday connections and animacy of the landscape, became suddenly apparent. I realised that in some ways, I was leaning to do similar, when I noticed the shalder's alarm call or the sight of diving gulls drew my gaze to the water. Often I couldn't identify the cause of these behaviours, but sometimes they revealed a bonxie overhead or an otter moving silently along the ebb. With the guidance of my neighbours, I was learning ways of noticing that opened up new understandings of place.

The constant chatter and fast-moving shapes of the tirricks were such a presence they drew my gaze, but I knew that if I got too close, they would attack, swooping down, their sharp beaks an effective weapon against intruders. I learned that if I stuck to the sheep paths that wound their way along the coastline the terns largely ignored me. However, if my feet strayed even a little from the path, piercing screams would fill the air as one or two birds flew towards me, hovering above until I returned to the path and continued on my way.

One day, Lowrie and Ina were talking about the terns, watching as they circled over the remains of an old sheep dip. Lowrie said he thought the birds would have a difficult time because it had been a strange year. It was too wet, and island fishermen were saying mackerel weren't in their usual places. Ina agreed, saying it felt cold, as if the winter wind had never truly been away. 'Are there many tirrick eggs this year?' she asked Lowrie, who replied that he had not been to count them yet. 'I'll hae a look now,' he said, and invited me to watch.

As we walked over the rocks towards the headland, Lowrie explained that he had a look every year, but only once, as he didn't want to disturb the birds too much. Raising a stick above his head to ward off attacks, he cautioned me to stay directly behind him, only putting my feet exactly where he put his. As we drew closer the colony rose, a swirling mass of white against the blue sky, the chilling sound of their cries seeming to travel through my whole body. As Lowrie stopped and pointed towards the ground, two birds dived in quick succession, a dull thud indicating they had made contact with Lowrie's still-raised stick. I realised that the patch of ground Lowrie was pointing to was a nest. It was just a few strands of dried seaweed and some blades of yellowing grass, upon which rested two eggs, olive green with mottled brown spots. They were so perfectly camouflaged that when, moments later, I glanced behind me, I couldn't tell which part of the shoreline housed the nest.

Again and again Lowrie pointed, seeing nests long before they were visible to me, and I understood that I could never come here myself. Even with the utmost care, I just didn't have the knowledge to not put these precious eggs in danger. I asked Lowrie how he saw them from such a distance and he explained the movements and calls of the birds alerted him to the fact he was close to a nest. He then scanned the rocks, looking for tell-tale shapes, the patterns of deliberate activity distinct from how the seaweed lies when it is blown by the wind. As we rounded the corner away from the colony, the birds began to settle, most returning to the rocks, while a few sentries circled, making sure we were truly gone.

I thought about all the signals, the ones we give and the ones we notice as we go through life. Thinking about these connections between attention and belonging brought me back to something that had been troubling me about island ponies and the upcoming shows. In some ways, breeders' comments seemed contradictory. Passages in my fieldnotes had question marks and scribbles in the margins, as I tried to make sense of assertions of the importance of meticulously planned breeding and the simultaneous feelings of surprise and apprehension that accompanied foaling time. Respecting ponies' choices seemed integral to daily practice on pony studs, and yet breeding decisions were often made with reference to seemingly abstract characteristics. Breeders all seemed to want very similar things for their ponies – correct conformation, good bone, nice colour – and yet wanted their ponies to be identifiable as their stud 'type'. The contrast between the establishment of breeds as a way to demonstrate and expand aristocratic control over land, and Shetland native breeds' role in challenging landlord control, was stark. And yet shows, where animal bodies were assessed according to human rules and ponies' owners were rewarded, appeared to exemplify domestication as human domination.

Genealogies of pedigree breeds are very similar to the aristocratic family trees designed to demonstrate their 'good blood' precisely because the same ideas of breeding and descent informed the first stud-books. Margaret Derry, in her book *Bred for Perfection*, describes how during the nineteenth century, breed shows became a popular way for people to publicise the results of their breeding practices. Such shows encouraged people to experiment more with breeding, transforming shapes, sizes, colours, often resulting in individual animals that appeared significantly different from other members of the same species. However, although the recognised number of breeds was increasing, strict rules relating to the characteristics permitted within each breed worked to reduce diversity, since breeders were rewarded for producing animals that closely fitted specified breed criteria. Although in many ways animals were centre stage in these events, paraded, judged and photographed, they were often treated more as objects than as sentient beings.

Within the context of shows, pedigree breeders were

viewed as architects, realising their artistic designs by moulding animal bodies into desired forms. And yet, as the months passed and I spent more time with people and ponies, I began to think about how Tim Ingold considers the practices of architecture. In his book *Making*, he wrote that we often ignore the processes and materials involved in creating a building. Creativity is associated with the design stage, with making perceived as little more than implementing an already concrete plan. Once a design is completed, there is little attention given to how this creation responds and adapts as part of social life. Ingold draws our attention towards the activities and materials involved in the process of making, so that rather than seeing a designer as 'being aloof, imposing his designs on a world that is ready and waiting to receive them', we might recognise that the most a designer can do is 'intervene in worldly processes that are already going on, and which give rise to the forms of the living world that we see all around us'.

As the months passed and I watched people learning about their new foals and choosing the mares and stallions to place together, I began to understand this in relation to the interplay between design and improvisation, planning and making. It is in June and July that mares and stallions run together, to ensure that foals will be born in May of the next year. As I stood in the summer fields, breeders would tell me about why they had chosen their combinations. There were some ponies who had been together previously and had produced good results; others had physical attributes thought to complement each other, or they might have borrowed a stallion from another stud whose foals they admired.

Decisions about who would work well together permeated the whole year, as people learned about their new foals, watched ponies at shows, and decided who to buy and sell. This knowledge formed as part of breeders' skilled practice, where through their attention they learned to see not only the animal in front of them, but the potential futures that might come from them. Just as Ingold says that design is not separate from making, so breeding decisions cannot be separated from everyday lives with ponies. Knowledge is developed through embodied practice, and so ponies must be considered active participants in breeding practices.

The social life of bloodlines

Ideas of stud type, of belonging, were necessarily subjective and difficult to define, as they were formed through years, and sometimes generations, of breeding practice. The importance of good bone or intelligence was something all breeders agreed upon, and yet what this meant to each person, and how it was recognised, varied considerably. June's diagram of bloodlines, which on the surface may seem to echo the strict framework of pedigree breeding, was, in practice, a living document, where past, present and future merged.

'I ken what I am breeding,' she told me, 'especially the Berry line, right back to Spangle o' Berry, an' back, an' back, an' back, aw that ponies is in my living memory and I can mind them aw, and I can mind what foals they left and what they were like.' As I visited June regularly throughout fieldwork I watched her relationship with two young horses develop. June loved Sula before she even met her. Showing me a picture of a piebald filly for sale she said she just knew she was 'one of mine'.

The foal's bloodlines could be traced to Urban of Knowe, June's old stallion who is admired and respected across Shetland. But it wasn't just that: many foals' breeding could be traced back to this stallion and she doesn't want to buy them all; rather it was a combination of that and something else. June tried to explain this something to me, drawing my attention to the foal's stance and expression, how you could just tell she was a character, before repeating that she could just tell she was 'one of mine'.

In contrast, June had always appeared unsure about Haeva's place. When I first met June, she'd introduced me to Haeva, whose strength and movement she admired but who she felt acted too flighty. Suspecting Haeva's fieldmate may have been winding her up, June moved her to a field with Sula, the foal, and Toni, her oldest and wisest mare. She chose a field near her house so she could watch them closely.

One sunny afternoon when I visited June we sat outside with the ponies. June said that Sula, as expected, was instantly at home. She was laidback while also being attentive and respectful towards Toni, and wasn't taking any of *her* nonsense June said, gesturing to Haeva. Rather than calming down in her new field, Haeva was appearing increasingly frantic. 'She just isn't learning,' June said sadly. 'Has she not got the sense to learn from Toni? Is this just her personality?'

'Watch this,' June said and she placed three piles of food on the ground. Sula and Toni quickly chose a pile and began to eat. But Haeva appeared restless, starting to chew at some food before moving towards the other ponies. June voiced Haeva's thoughts using a high-pitched, panicked voice: 'Ooooh ! What's she got? Better check!' Then, as she moved towards Toni, who shood her away: 'Oooh! Oooh! Why's she kicking me in the face?!' And as she raced towards Sula's food: 'Oooh! Oooh! What's over here?' Despite being younger, June said, Sula showed more sense, moving to the vacated feed pile or approaching Toni and seeming to ask politely, 'Please can I have some?'

June sighed as she watched them. 'I hate seein' her that way.'

After she had finished eating, Sula came over to June, who took out a brush and started to groom her, continually talking to the foal in low, gentle tones. As the brush got deep under her coat, Sula began to move her lips. 'Whar's you snoot?' June laughed, as the foal turned her nose towards her and began to groom her in return. 'This is what I want,' June said. 'A laidback pony that wants to spend time with me, laidback but with sense aboot them.' She watched Haeva sadly. 'She is a fine-lookin' horse. I'll try her up in the hill. See if she learns onything from being wi a herd.'

Several years later, as I was writing up my PhD thesis, I sent June the section I'd written on Haeva and she wrote back and updated me on her:

Haeva is still here and had her first foal this year. I must give her credit as she's been a fantastic first-time mother, but it has been very interesting to observe that her foal has spent more time with the other ponies than with her, almost using her as a milk bar but little else. Not surprisingly, he latched on to that same old piebald mare who teaches everyone, and her black daughter who is pretty wise too. I see absolutely nothing of his mother in him – he's almost like a clone of the rest ... Is this genetic or a result of his upbringing, who knows? The mare herself is slightly better but still nuts. Knocked me over in the quarry today at feeding time in her hurry to escape from a set of flying feet! She'll be sold next year.

Belonging is a far more social process than theories of pedigree breeding allow for. It is multi-layered and based on mutual recognition. When people place a mare and a stallion together, they have certain hopes based on the attributes of both parents and their plans for a stud 'type', but much of the joy of breeding comes from the unknown, from the hope of producing foals who *belong* to the stud. I saw how each stud had their favourite foals, those who stood out as special, the ones that drew their eye, the ones they would never sell. These foals would be kept and used for breeding once they were old enough, their name, body and personality contributing to the stud's next generation.

Often, as it was with June and Sula, the attraction was instant, then built and reinforced through their experiences together. These favourite foals were often compared to those who had come before, from stud or island history. Some known from direct experience, others from family stories. Summer days with foals, winter storms and hill herds, this is how ponies become known, loved and respected. This is not simply humans choosing arbitrary characteristics and then controlling animal reproduction to realise these goals: this is an engaged, reciprocal and intrinsically social practice. Of course, there are limits to ponies' choices – mares and stallions are not free to reproduce unchecked – but there is far more room for equine autonomy than traditional narratives of domestication imply. Belonging is not something decided by people, it is an engaged social practice where identities, human and equine, emerge in relation to each other. It is a process that Donna J. Haraway, in her book *When Species Meet*, describes as 'becoming with' the animals we love, where 'the partners do not precede their relating'.

Through her attention, June learned from each pony their personality and preferences, but also reinforced ideas about what it meant for a horse to be 'one of mine'. Through these experiences people are shaped, learning who they are as they share their lives with animals, their own identity as a pony breeder emerging through everyday encounters. In pony breeding, as with everything in life, we become who we are through our experiences with others. It is something often acknowledged in our human relationships – our friends, family or work colleagues – but the effects of non-humans are often considered as somehow less generative.

Some fascinating new studies have revealed some of the visible physical transformations that motherhood has on the brain, reshaping responses to stimuli, affecting how and who we are in the world. Although limited in scope, mostly focusing on those who had physically carried and given birth to their children, there is strong evidence of the same changes in the brain structure of adoptive mothers. Thus demonstrating the physical effects of the social act of parenting. So many studies on the effects of our environment on us focus on specific life processes, particularly pregnancy and motherhood, and yet the implications go far further. If love, and our experiences with certain people, shape our bodies and minds, then surely our other relationships, those with more than human worlds, also affect who we are.

Being a pony breeder is such an important part of people's lives. There is, of course, all the hard work that comes with the everyday running of a stud, but there is also the more diffuse attention. Noticing the shape of a pony on the hill, recognising or wondering whose horse it is, seeing how they are faring in the day's weather. The feeling of connection to history, watching ponies graze in places where horses have been for generations, or the joy of putting horses into the place where your grandparents' horses grazed. Through this attention, the practice of breeding shapes relationships with Shetland, extending home out beyond houses and gardens to include landscapes and animals. This identity is always in a process of becoming, as people become who they are with the animals and landscapes they love.

The garden

One morning, as I was hanging out the laundry, Ina told me that Yoda often followed her as she walked on the ness. She thought he seemed interested in the sheep, describing how he sometimes looked between her and them, as if struggling to choose who to go with. A few times, when she'd been hanging out laundry, she'd thought she'd seen him with the flock, confirming this identification with her binoculars. I was delighted to hear this as I had been worrying about Yoda. When I walked with him to the sheep he was still largely running up to them and being butted away. Sometimes he tried to butt them back, lowering his tiny head in an act of bravery or defiance. Recently he had started trying to mount them, gripping tight with his forelegs as the startled recipients of his advances fled. Yoda had been castrated soon after he'd been born, so I asked Lowrie about his behaviour. He reassured me that this was quite normal: lambs often did this with each other, and because Yoda had no lamb friends this was how he was with the sheep. As I watched him, I felt heartbroken for this lonely lamb, trying to interact with sheep but having his advances rejected, while seemingly unaware of, and completely unresponsive to, their gestures of friendship.

If we are always becoming through the process of life, could he learn to become a sheep? Would the instincts that caused him to follow sheep paths and seek milk from yowes increase with time? Or would he always be stuck in between, not part of sheep worlds but also without a definite place with humans? I thought of my own becoming. Since moving to Shetland, I had felt a significant change in myself. Perhaps this was less of an abrupt change and more of a shift in focus, a form of re-engaging. So much of island life, attention to the weather, the presence of history and networks of community, felt so natural that it was more like remembering than learning anew. The dialect in particular was weaving its way through my thoughts. The light haze of distant rain was now a 'smir', a foal kicking up its heels as it pranced was being 'filskit', and if I made a sudden move that startled the seals I had 'gluffed' them. Words from the south, with which I was more familiar, just couldn't capture the feel of phenomena in the same way, but I was unsure about my right to use local dialect. Shetland once had a distinct language called Norn, a derivative of Old Norse. With the architects of Scottish colonialism, as it was across the world, came attempts to suppress the local language and punish those using it. Over time the Norn language ceased to be used but a distinct island dialect remains. I worried if I were to use these words, as someone from Scotland, it would be seen as uninformed appropriation.

Very little had emerged from the earth of my vegetable patch, despite everybody else's potatoes and carrots visibly growing and some already harvested. I had been fighting a losing battle against the rain, digging and deepening the ditches each time the ground appeared waterlogged, but although the water flowed away, the soil remained wet and heavy. Robbie said that more rain had been forecast so I should try to lift the tatties soon. Tentatively, I dug around the small patches of green leaves and looked underneath. Below each seed tatty were tiny, marble-sized potatoes, green and inedible. I sifted through the muddy sludge to see if anything else was hidden below but there was nothing. I pulled the carrots from the ground. Each one was pencil thin and more yellow than orange. Looking at the tufts of leaves aboveground, they seemed close together, and I realised I probably should have thinned them out more. I felt disappointed and deflated – I had nothing to show for all my hard work and no produce to offer to neighbours, a gesture that had felt so important, to make something that I could share with everyone who had been so kind to me.

Increasing pregnancy sickness was making things harder, causing me to draw back, making me feel less able to join in activities. It was partly the physical effects: after a long day of fieldwork my exhaustion was so consuming that the thought of going to the heritage club or joining neighbours in the pub seemed like too much. I kept telling myself that I would rest that night and do something the next day, but each day brought more tiredness. But I reasoned that the sickness should start abating soon; I was getting close to twelve weeks and would soon be able to share my news.

The shows

The day of the Walls Show was grey, with low clouds draped across hilltops and so much moisture in the atmosphere that the world felt full of perpetual drizzle. Approaching the showground, my first thoughts were how underwhelming it seemed. The large field was split into two rings for the ponies, surrounding which were temporary metal enclosures where the animals stood to wait their turn. To the left were the sheep pens, some of them already decorated with bright-coloured rosettes, indicating judging had commenced. Around the pens, men in boiler suits, wellies and flat caps spoke to each other in low tones, writing notes on their show programmes. Despite the early hour and the weather, there was already a long, waterproof-adorned queue for Mr Stripey, Shetland's only ice cream van. Bleats, whinnies and the clanking of hoofs against metal merged with the sounds from the tannoy, which was blaring out Metallica's 'Fade to Black'.

I joined Jackie and started to work with her to prepare the ponies. The first classes were children's ridden and lead rein. I watched as a very young child, neatly dressed in jodhpurs and hacking jacket, rode a small grey pony around the ring. When I next looked they were standing by the pens. The pony appeared asleep on her feet, her bottom lip brushing the grass as she snoozed while her rider chatted excitedly, holding the rosette they had won.

The pens were a flurry of activity as everybody brushed their ponies, removing any trace of mud or stray hair before spraying them with coat shine and oiling their hoofs. I smiled as I saw Bjørn, who was also a hairdresser, take a comb out of his back pocket and use it to neaten up one of his ponies. The work felt like an uphill struggle, and a combination of bending, the smell of conditioner and nerves meant my nausea was worse than ever. As I groomed Ellen, Midnight, who was due in the ring first and had been perfectly prepared, pooped and stepped in it before I could clean it up. I was still desperately rubbing her legs and tail with a damp cloth as Jackie pinned a number to my arm and told me to get into the ring.

The judge stood in the middle of the ring as ponies and handlers entered and started walking slowly around in a circle. Remembering with trepidation how she had pulled and escaped my grasp just weeks before, I was relieved as Midnight walked nicely, ears pricked, looking relaxed but interested. When we were asked to trot, Midnight pulled forward slightly before settling into a comfortable pace. All the ponies were asked to stand in a line as the judge called us forward one by one, to stand in front of her, then walk and trot along the centre of the ring. It took a little jostling for me to get Midnight to stand square, but she did, and when we returned to the line of ponies, I felt like I had done a pretty good job for my first time.

The pace of the show felt relentless, each class immediately following the one before with no time to catch my breath in between. Some of Jackie's other ponies won rosettes, but it was Tawney who was the star, winning class after class, beaten only in the final championship by Bjørn's beautiful stallion. I felt so proud of this little horse who had danced around the ring, interested and alert, and who was now enthusiastically chewing on one of the many rosettes lining her pen.

Once the pony classes were over, I had a chance to look around the show. The queue for Mr Stripey was now even longer and included several men in full Viking attire whom I assumed must be part of an Up Helly Aa fire festival squad. Large marquees contained stalls selling local produce, raffles, competitions for the children and, rather confusingly, a life-size plastic cow with udders that could be milked. I was surprised by the sheer number of people. Only two of the summer shows, the Viking Shetland Pony Show and the Cunningsburgh Show, allow entries from across Shetland. In the others, entries are limited to the area that the show is held in. Despite this, there were people from all over Shetland there to see what ponies other studs were showing. Hazy sunlight began to break through the clouds, and there was a real holiday feel to the day as folk milled around chatting to friends and neighbours. The air was filled with stories: descriptions of how a favourite pony was bought, the antics of foals, laments over the weather, and hopes for a successful show season.

The other shows passed in a similar way. Early starts, hard work, but thankfully I was able to show all the ponies Jackie brought, and although lacking the skills of more experienced handlers, I felt I had done an adequate job. As I drove away from the Viking show, the final show of the season, I felt relieved it was all over. With some time to spare before my ferry booking, I went for a walk along the coast, enjoying the quiet after such a busy week. I looked over the water towards a broch, which still stands at over 13 metres tall, and dominates the landscape of the tiny island of Mousa. This tower features in Viking sagas, as a refuge for eloping lovers and as the place of siege in 1153, when Earl Harald Maddadsson attacked the structure to rescue his mother who was captive inside. Although I could not see them from this distance, the broch is now home to thousands of storm petrels. These tiny birds, distantly related to the albatross, return each year to breed within the ancient walls.

Walking further along the water's edge, I came to the remains of another broch. Now only a few feet high, these circular walls would once have stood as tall as those on the island opposite, the broch's twin. As is common in Shetland, with few sources of quality stone, older buildings were often dismantled so their stone could be reused. Beside where the broch had once stood were the remains of crofthouses. In the mid-1800s, forty-three people had lived here, a flour-ishing community, until changing economic patterns, and the Clearances, led to people leaving this place. Around the lichen-covered walls sheep grazed, and in one of the windowsills a fulmar chick watched me from the safety of its nest.

I sat among the old stones, evidence of centuries of life still providing shelter for wild birds and domestic sheep. Suddenly, I felt the exertion of the previous days catching up with me. My limbs and back ached and I was so tired it was as if my body were being dragged unwillingly towards sleep. But amidst the exhaustion I felt proud; I knew I had shown Jackie's ponies well. Several breeders had told me I had done a good job, and some had even enlisted my help with their own ponies when I wasn't in the ring. By the end of the final show Jackie had been talking about me helping her next year, saying I could perhaps even show some of her more difficult-to-handle horses. I was so relieved that I hadn't made any mistakes, that I had done what was expected of me, but it was more than that. During the shows I had felt I was truly part of things, that I knew what I was doing and I was being useful. While some elements of fitting in to island life were going less well, here, with the ponies, I was beginning to feel more comfortable, like I belonged. I drove home with a renewed enthusiasm, thinking about my fieldwork time that remained, confident that I was improving my skills both as an anthropologist and as a competent helper at the pony studs. By the time I approached the ferry terminal the light was golden and the sky was the colour of fire. I checked the time: at just after 9pm it seemed too early for sunset, and I realised with a shock that the seasons were once again changing. Summer was coming to an end.

7

HOSPITAL

I LAY ON THE BED as cold jelly was squeezed onto my stomach. The room was dark and my body tensed as I waited, hoped, to see my baby on the screen. I could picture it in my mind, a familiar sight from friends' Facebook posts, and I couldn't wait to have a photo of my own baby to take home. My chest tightened as the midwife said nothing but pressed the ultrasound device deeper into my skin. I tried to stay calm but as the silence continued I cried, 'What's wrong?' hoping for an answer other than what now felt inevitable.

'How many weeks do you think you are?' the midwife asked, and I replied, 'Thirteen. Is there a baby? Is there a heartbeat?'

She frowned slightly, looking at the screen, and said, 'I can see *something* . . .' With those words, I knew my pregnancy had ended. Following an internal scan, she confirmed that the baby had died some time ago but my body had failed to recognise this. 'Would you like some time alone?' she asked, and Steve, ashen-faced, nodded.

I slipped off the bed and crumpled on the floor, my head on Steve's lap. There were no tears, everything had stopped, it made no sense. I have no idea how long we sat like this, without words. I knew I needed to leave the room, but other women were waiting for their appointments, to see their babies, and I couldn't bear to walk past them. The midwife returned with leaflets to explain our options. She told me that another scan was required later to confirm some details, so I'd need to return to hospital in the afternoon. I had no idea this was not standard practice.

As soon as the car door closed behind me the tears started. I felt trapped. All I wanted was to go home to bed, but because of the second scan I needed to stay on the mainland. Steve suggested we drive to St Ninian's Isle. I protested: this was where we had planned to go to celebrate seeing our baby for the first time. Now that dream had died. But we couldn't stay parked at the hospital and needed to go somewhere, so off we drove. I sat, looking out to the long stretch of golden sand that joins St Ninian's Isle to the mainland. This was somewhere that I had always felt held magic and mystery, the remains of ancient chapels telling of centuries of worship concentrated in this place. In the 1950s a schoolboy discovered a wooden box containing a horde of Pictish treasure and the jawbone of a porpoise. It is a place where the past seemed closer, existing alongside you. Exploring the island, weaving a path between rabbit holes while trying not to startle the island's sheep, you never knew what you might discover.

On this day, I couldn't leave the car. I looked down over the beach, watching the waves come to shore as the strong wind sent clouds racing across the sky, illuminating the families playing on the beach, before suddenly plunging them into shadow. This world suddenly felt small and distant, as if I was separated by an invisible membrane. I could not make sense of what had happened. The awareness of a dead baby still inside me felt too much to bear. I had worried throughout the pregnancy and yet my body had seemed to provide reassurance that everything was OK. Each week my pregnancy symptoms had increased, telling me that of course there was a baby, otherwise why would I feel this way? I kept repeating these statements out loud, desperate and nonsensical. This day should have been so different. We should have been on the beach, exploring and celebrating the potential for new life, not mourning the death of what had never been. Slowly the sun got closer to the horizon and the light started to fade. Finally, it was time to go back to the maternity department.

I lay on the bed again. Another internal scan, this time more uncomfortable, more insistent. A second midwife explained kindly that it would take some time but they needed to get a good look. A part of me kept hoping that there was a mistake, that they would indeed find a heartbeat. Even though I knew this couldn't be true, I could not shut off this stupid, desperate hope. The two midwives looked at the screen. The silence in the room was occasionally broken by the sickening sound of photographs being taken inside me. I panicked, desperate for them to stop looking, to stop taking pictures of it. I wanted to escape, to run and not come back, but I knew that any movement from me would make the process longer and more difficult. So I stayed still and waited.

I hadn't really expected more bad news that day, and was completely unprepared when I was told there were complications. I tried to follow what they were saying as they explained that it was likely a partial molar pregnancy, where two sperm simultaneously fertilised one egg, resulting in a foetus that could never become a live baby but could potentially develop into cancer. I would need to be flown to Aberdeen to have surgery to ensure that everything was removed. There would also be a period of follow-up, potentially as long as a year, to make sure there was no sign of cancer developing. When I learned that getting pregnant was not safe during this monitoring time I felt even more hopeless.

The week I spent in Aberdeen was the most difficult time of my life. A series of mistakes and miscommunications led to several more scans than were medically necessary, each scan another painful, shocking reminder that it was still there. Its presence made me sick. I wanted it gone, but over and over, surgery was delayed. Diagnoses were changed and most of the time Steve and I were alone in a hospital room with no idea what was happening. Finally, the surgery was complete, I was groggy, tearful and in pain, yet somehow I felt a little better, one step closer to recovery.

There was some time before our flight home and so we walked the familiar streets near where we'd once lived, through the park where we'd spent some of our first dates. There was a feel of autumn. Reds and yellows joined the green on the trees and the still air had a slight frost-like bite. These places were familiar. I'd lived in Aberdeen for seven years, far longer than I had been in Shetland, yet, as I walked, it felt alien. The grey buildings, so similar to one another, stood cold and aloof, a stark contrast to Shetland houses that each had their own personality. Trees and buildings obscured most of the sky that now appeared, distant, somehow abstract, compared to the ever-changing Shetland skies, so alive and intimate. The noise and smell of the traffic unsettled me and the faces that passed were blank, unsmiling. My desperation to leave and return to Shetland grew.

The flight back was beautiful. The blue sky above us was filled with small, white, puffy clouds. Looking down, more of these clouds against the blue of the sea made the distinction between up and down, sea and sky, seem irrelevant. As the plane lowered, the sea got gradually closer, the froth-tipped waves clearly visible. Familiar shapes came into view, the cliffs at Sumburgh Head and the green treeless expanse of the south mainland. As the passengers stepped out onto the runway, most rushed, heads down, into the terminal building to escape the wind. I stood for a moment, feeling the wind, a living connection between sea and sky. Taking a deep breath, I walked towards the terminal building, relieved to be home.

Although the sights and sounds of Shetland made me feel instantly more relaxed, I was also a little uneasy. I did not want to return to the cold anonymity of Aberdeen, but for the first time, Whalsay felt claustrophobic. The proximity of my neighbours and the culture of taking an interest in the lives of others had until this point felt nice, safe and warm. Now I just wanted to be left alone. People knew I had been to hospital but I had not said what for. Despite knowing that miscarriage was common, that it was rarely, if ever, caused by the actions of the mother, I still felt inexplicable shame and guilt. I didn't want anybody to know. Looking back, I wish I had just said. People would have been kind and supportive, and I probably really needed this companionship. Instead, I stayed silent about why I had been away, and as a result felt an oppressive need to pretend I was fine whenever I met people. This self-imposed pressure caused me to try to avoid people, slipping out of the house quietly, hoping I would not meet anyone on my walks, hurrying away after just a few words if I did.

Outside was where I needed to be, it was where I could heal and start to make sense of things. As soon as I got home, I walked out onto the ness, feeling the welcome presence of wind and sea. Immediately the tears started to flow, as I remembered all that I had experienced here: the whales, porpoises, storms, sunsets and rainbows. I had been so excited at the thought of introducing this beautiful world to a new life. But now I felt empty. Despite its beauty, it seemed far away, somehow separate. I could see it but not feel it. Yoda appeared from nowhere, galloping full-speed towards me, *baa*-ing loudly and insistently. I bent down, longing for a hug. Unfortunately, Yoda had stopped accepting hugs when he was a week old. Wild-eyed, he pawed at me, looking for the sheep nuts he knew were in my pocket. I stroked his soft fleece as he ate the nuts. He nuzzled at my leg and followed me for a short time as I walked, but then returned to the flock, following them as they grazed. Smiling slightly through my tears, I wondered if my time away might have been good for him, made him more sheep-like.

I walked on the ness every day. My mind swirled with questions, hopes and worries. Would I ever be able to get pregnant again? When would the doctors say it was safe to try again? And what if the same thing happened? My memories of the summer seemed tainted. All that time I'd thought life was growing inside me, a tiny invisible companion, yet that pregnancy had never, could never have, made a living baby. I felt sick as I thought how I had talked to it, loved it, this thing that had never existed. Just a lie my body had told. I was angry, hating my body with every step, resentful of the signs of pregnancy that remained. I walked, head down, seeing little. Feeling dizzy, I sat for a moment on a rock, and realised while fighting to hold back tears that I was also holding my breath. I noticed my clenched fists, the tightness in my jaw. I tried to relax my mind, looking to sea and sky, trying to be still in the moment, but as I took my first deep breath my phone rang. An Aberdeen number. My heart sank: it was the hospital again. Since coming home I was getting regular calls about test results, requests for blood and urine samples, intrusive questions but few answers. Each difficult conversation felt like it was dragging me back to the hospital, reigniting fear and worry, making it impossible to escape.

Slowly, as it always does, the world started to creep back into my consciousness. The call of an oyster-catcher, a glimpse of an otter, or the sheep walking in formation towards the beach could all momentarily distract me from my thinking. But it was the wind that really started to heal me. One evening, a few weeks after I came home, it gathered in intensity, the sheep sheltered under the peat banks, their actions alerting me to the approaching storm. From my bed I listened to rain battering the windows and the low howl of the wind. At dawn I walked on the ness, staggering against the force of the gale. A ceiling of low cloud with no end in sight was in constant motion, trapping all light beneath its shroud. The sodden landscape below seemed to glow slightly, filling the world with a green-ish, otherworldly light. A turquoise sea churned. Waves gained momentum as they got closer to shore, their white frothy tips blown back by the gale to form a misty haze above the water. Gulls wheedled above the waves, battered and blown off course by gusts of wind, their cries unheard against the constant roar of the sea.

The wind matched my mood: frantic, multi-directional and angry. Yet at the same time, I felt its calming influence. I was suddenly present in the landscape in a way I had not been for weeks, perhaps even months, as I began to realise that for much of my pregnancy I had started retreating inwards, caught up inside my own body and tortured by a mind full of worries. Just as I felt the elements, this reminder of the beauty, pain and continuity that is life, a movement caught my eye. A tiny bobbing shape. Instantly I got low to the ground and slowly moved closer. It was a goldcrest, blown in with the storm. Despite the gale I could hear its high-pitched musical notes as it hopped towards me. Another appeared behind it, then another, six in total, each one stopping occasionally to peck at the ground before moving forward as a group, continually calling to each other. Time stopped. I lay on the sodden ground. The gold and red of their heads the brightest colour in the landscape and their song somehow louder than the gale surrounding us, they moved towards me. They were close enough to touch, those beautiful, delicate birds. As quickly as they arrived, they disappeared over the brow of a hill, their song audible even when they were out of sight. I stayed still long after they had gone, the moment seemed so unreal. I walked home feeling like a weight had lifted. Although things were the same as they had been the day before, somehow, everything felt different.

Such moments made me wonder about the world

and our relationships with it. How the things we notice can slowly or immediately change us. Often, when I lived in cities, at times I'd felt upset or overwhelmed, I'd felt the world intervene. A deer and fawn grazing beneath a railway bridge, unseen by those above them; a fox joining me on my walk home, an unexpected but welcome companion, or the dazzling brightness of a butterfly visiting flowers growing from soot-coated walls. Moments that could transform my thinking, remind me of the world and its possibilities, causing me to look outward. Those moments, and so many more like them, became woven into my experiences and memories, part of my story, and yet they were also part of the everyday and often unnoticed parts of city streets. Deer, foxes and flowers were not so unusual that seeing them was necessarily an event, yet each of those times it felt different, like a form of communication, the world showing me what I needed to see, reminding me of its presence, of the links between things.

The sale

The pony sale in Lerwick took place soon after my discharge from hospital, before either my mind or body were ready. I felt weak and ill-prepared, and even before my miscarriage I had watched the sale date approach with trepidation. Although the sale was an opportunity for prospective buyers to see the range and quality of Shetland ponies from Shetland, it was also where ponies might be sold for low prices, onward to uncertain futures. The 'meat man' stalked stories of the sale: people and companies who would buy the unwanted ponies to sell as petfood on international markets.

There has been an annual sale of Shetland ponies in Lerwick since 1959, with significant variation in prices reflecting the changing popularity of the breed. In recent decades sale prices have remained low. In the months preceding the sale, as people sat with their foals, the next generations of their studs, we were joined by the spectre of uncertainty and loss, the possibility of a sad goodbye. When foals remained unsold, or were sold at low prices, it raised questions about the future of the breed. Most breeders had reduced the numbers of foals they bred each year and had sought to achieve a balance between breeding the type of pony they loved and ensuring their foals had the greatest chance of finding a good home. Hopes, history, responsibility to the lives of their foals, and responses to external market demands flowed through everyday decisions, which the event of this annual sale brought into sharp focus.

I stepped into the mart's café. It was warm, and groups of people sat around small tables with chequered cloths. The air was filled with the smells of breakfast cooking. As more people arrived they greeted folk they knew with a wave, smile or a quick chat, before heading through a door at the back of the room. Each time, as the door opened, sounds of clanging metal and high-pitched whinnying joined the murmur of voices. With a Styrofoam cup of lukewarm tea in one hand, and the sale programme in the other, I ventured through, to see the ponies.

Before entering the sale ring, ponies waited in a large concrete room. Metal hurdles separated the area into pens, with corridors running alongside so people could see all the ponies. There were Shetland ponies of all ages, sizes and colours, each wearing a sticker that displayed their lot number. As torrential rain bounced noisily off the corrugated roof, I bent down to speak to two timid-looking foals. One moved forward tentatively and sniffed my hand before moving back towards the corner of the pen. I checked their number in the sale catalogue and realised with a shock that I knew these foals. I had seen them several times, bounding and playing in the summer sun. Today I didn't recognise them. They seemed so small.

As I walked around the room, I tried to ignore Inga but found myself drawn to her pen. She lifted her head as I approached and nuzzled my hand in greeting. I'd met Inga in early spring, when visiting the Gue stud, and had felt an instant connection to her. Mid-size, grey, with a very pretty face, she seemed wise and gentle as she grazed next to me, occasionally rubbing her head up against my leg. 'Looking for food!' Carole had laughed, saying Inga was a lovely example of the old-type Shetland pony, incredibly gentle and the perfect child's pony. Soon after I'd discovered I was pregnant I'd seen her listed in the sale catalogue and it had seemed like fate. The sale would fall not long after my twelve-week scan, and I'd planned to buy her for my unborn baby. A sudden sense of loss hit me and, fighting back the tears, I turned away from Inga and scanned the room, trying to keep myself in the moment by noticing the details.

The room was in constant motion as people added the finishing touches to get their ponies ready for the ring. This activity reminded me of the summer shows, yet the atmosphere was completely different. There were fewer smiles, conversations were brief and tense, and the regular bouts of raucous laughter that usually punctuate pony events were absent. As I watched, I noticed the time owners took with their ponies, a quiet word, a scratch behind their ears, and sometimes a hug or a kiss. These brief moments of affection between pony and owner were among my favourite parts of life in Shetland. As I spent time with practical crofting people, who on the surface may seem as far removed from sentimentality as it is possible to get, these moments of familiarity showed the deep love and respect they have for their animals.

It is the actions of the ponies as much as those of the humans that reveal this love. I remembered one spring day, a breeder telling me the history of the breed and the importance of correct breeding practice. He was speaking in a very earnest, professional way. It was clearly important to him that I understood and remembered the facts he was telling me, as he knew I would be representing Shetland ponies through my work. As he spoke, more and more of his ponies gathered around him. Initially he'd tried to ignore them and keep talking to me, but it was clear they were not used to such a cold response. They'd come closer, circling him and nuzzling at his clothes. Before long he was absentmindedly giving them a pat and animatedly telling me stories about them. I smiled at this memory of love for these ponies, but almost instantly the sadness returned. Today, these moments had a different feel. As I looked around, each person in their own way was saying goodbye to a horse they cared for, that they might never hear from again.

As I entered the sale room I was surprised at the number of empty seats. I recognised the majority of people present as those who had come with ponies. Mary from Burland Croft was standing by the ring, and she said sadly, 'This is nothing compared to how it used to be. It was always a social occasion, where everybody went for their Shetland pony, and now ...' Her voice trailed off as she looked around the sparsely occupied room.

Although the sale appeared poorly attended, there were many bids, and as I listened to the conversations circling the hall I learned some of the ponies sold were destined for new homes hundreds of miles away. The recent addition of i-bidder, which allows potential buyers to watch and bid from anywhere in the world, was raising hopes about the future of the sale.

The auctioneer's voice rang out, his words mostly incomprehensible to me, a lilting rhythm of numbers, adjusting higher or lower, responding to signals from the stands that I could not see. I watched closely, noticing that a movement of the sale catalogue or the slightest incline of a head was enough for his trained eye to recognise a bid. If a pony didn't make its reserve, he would look to the owner, who would say whether they would sell at the lower cost. Several breeders appeared tearful as they led their ponies around, unsure who was bidding or where their horse's new home would be.

A boat trip

One evening, a few days after the sale, Steve and I were invited to join our neighbour James on a fishing trip. I enthusiastically accepted, but within minutes began to worry about what I had agreed to. Although I was coming to terms with the loss, my feelings were still hard to predict, and out of nowhere tears could fall, sudden and unstoppable. On a boat there was nowhere to hide. I felt I should perhaps have declined the offer.

The boat glided on velvet sea, the stillness of the day and the patchwork sky reflected in the water, shades of silvery blue, darker and lighter in places, with barely a ripple on its surface. As I looked back on the place that had been my home for the last nine months, I was forcefully struck by how small this smattering of houses looked, surrounded by sea and peat hill. Yet it didn't look lonely, it seemed safe and self-contained. I imagined how it would have been years ago: before the roads and regular ferries, these small townships had to produce everything they needed, but even then, the island was never isolated. Like everywhere in Shetland, the sea connected the people and the place to distant worlds through trade and exploration.

As we moved further away from the main island, we passed several smaller islands, each with a story: of stones thrown up from the sea through a hole in the ground, unexpected and dangerous; legends of buried bodies, their origins forgotten, and the hardy sheep able to survive unattended with no known source of fresh water. The boat drew closer to an island; the steep sides were jagged and grey, slate-like, with patches of dusky pink or green where mosses and lichen grew. Scarfs perched on the edges, watching us, and a faint smell of guano lingered in the air. The gentle lapping of the waves against the rocks sounded different, gurgling, echoing and splashing into a deep, dark cave in the side of the rock. As we approached the entrance, it appeared vast, corridor-like. 'It runs through the whole island,' we were told, before the heart-stopping 'In we go!' Laughing at the looks on our faces, our skipper turned the boat around, and continued out to sea.

It was impossible to know which way to look. On one side was Noss, distant and looming; closer were groups of small rocky islands and the skerries, looking too small for human habitation. Curious seals followed alongside, and everywhere, the sky. The sun was lowering, throwing beams of golden light over the water, and the sky was alive with swirls of clouds, moved by distant winds that I could not feel. Occasionally, James said an area of water was 'good for mackerel' or 'perfect for creels'. I could see no difference between these places and the rest of the sea that surrounded us. James told me how knowledge of fishing grounds is passed down through generations, that his father and grandfather had taught him where to fish when he joined them on the boats as a child. They'd showed him how to notice the land to remember places at sea, identifying meids, or markers, to orientate him. When you discover a good place to fish, you look out for particular points on land – when the chimney of a certain building lines up with the cairn on top of the hill, or when you are in line between the points of two islands. This practice allows for identification of the same place in future. Some meids are public knowledge, their names on island maps; others are known only to the families who use them.

Groups of gannets flew past, amazingly close, their white bodies and yellow heads glowing in the fading light. We approached some bright-coloured buoys that revealed the presence of submerged lobster creels. The first few creels landed on the boat with a thump; several small crabs peered out at us before being tossed back into the water without a second glance. The next held a beautiful lobster, its huge claws gripping the mesh, its body shiny, dark blue with a purplish sheen, red antennae constantly in motion. It was lifted out carefully, measured and assessed as too small, and re-leased back into the sea. I watched it descend, visible for a surprisingly long time as it sank into the depths. As all the creels were brought up they were placed, side by side, onto a thick metal shelf on the boat. The last few creels had some lobsters large enough to keep, and they were placed into a bucket of seawater where they sat, stationary, for the remainder of the journey.

The sky darkened to a deep gold, the clouds a pale salmon pink and the sea like moonstone. As we drifted slowly towards home, it was time to try for mackerel. The line, equipped with several hooks, was dipped into the sea: there was no motion. The line was pulled up empty and placed down again: still nothing. We moved along a little and repeated the practice. This time, the instant the line submerged, it was moving frantically, several fish attached to the hooks. I have never appreciated how beautiful mack-erel are. In the supermarket their skins are a dull grey; but alive, fresh from the sea, their bodies are vibrant shades of green, blue and purple. Each time I looked, the colours seemed to change. The fish flopped and gulped. A long knife, quickly and skilfully used, ended their lives. James cast the fillets into a waiting box and threw the rest to the sea, where gulls, knowing the signs of a successful catch, had started to gather.

It was almost dark as we returned to shore. My

worries about tears had proved unfounded. For the duration of the journey, I had barely thought about pregnancy. The sky and sea, fish and stories had consumed me. It was just a few months until I was due to leave Whalsay, to go back to Aberdeen and write up my PhD. The feeling that it was not right to go had been growing. A tangible sense of unease at the thought of leaving this life, to go back to something that, although was more familiar, somehow seemed strange, alien, disconnected. A life I could no longer understand. That evening, returning from the boat, filled with joy at our neighbour's kindness and the beauty of land and sea, I acknowledged for the first time that I would not be leaving Shetland when I was expected to. I didn't yet know how I would stay – the practicalities of finding work and writing my thesis far from the university – but I knew I would find a way.

8

SUGAR AND YUKON

A FEW DAYS AFTER THE Lerwick sale, Aberdeen had its Shetland pony sale. Jackie was travelling south for this sale and taking some of her ponies with her. She asked if I could come and help with catching them and transporting them to the ferry. When I arrived at her croft I explained I had recently been in hospital and might struggle with some of the more physical tasks, but I would do the best I could. Jackie immediately asked me what was wrong. I gave some general, indistinct answer about having had surgery but healing well. Rather than being discouraged by my evasiveness she asked what the surgery had been for. I hesitated, took a deep breath, and told her. In that moment I couldn't think of a lie, and realised I didn't really want to tell one anyway. She responded kindly, but thankfully didn't ask any more questions. We worked together to catch ponies in the field and lead them to the horsebox. Time passed quickly, as the physical work and need to concentrate on the movements and actions of the ponies filled my mind. It was a relief to be actually doing something. As we travelled towards the ferry with the first lot of ponies I looked out the window. The tops of the hills were obscured by mist and the greens of summer were slowly giving way to the browns and russets of autumn. Some small groups of sheep picked their way across the heather, but other than that the area appeared devoid of life.

Jackie was talking about one of her foals that had been born at the end of August. Yukon had been an accident. Usually mares and stallions are only placed together for short periods of time during the summer, to ensure that foals are born in May or early June. After returning from a trip away, Jackie had found one of her stallions had escaped and was with her mare Sugar. She'd quickly moved the stallion back to his correct field but it was too late. Now she had a foal that would only be a few months old as winter approached. Jackie said that there would be a lot of work to halter-train her and get her used to contact, and that winter, with the bad weather and mud, was not a good time for this. 'You can come and help if you like,' Jackie offered. 'It would be a good learning experience and might take your mind off things.' I was already enthusiastically agreeing when Jackie continued,

'Maybe, if you can find a field for them, they can stay with you in Whalsay.'

I came home exhausted but excited. How to find a field? I knew that it wouldn't be an easy task on Whalsay. Many crofters who don't keep ponies are wary about having them on their land. Ponies are thought to churn up the ground and break fences in a way that other livestock do not. So I spoke to my neighbours and asked around the island. Responses were non-committal: 'Thar'll be somewhere I doot,' 'I mibbie hae a field, but I micht be needing yon fur da yowes come spring. I'll let de ken.'

Weeks passed and I heard nothing more from anyone, until Lowrie came to my rescue once again. Pulling his car up alongside me as I walked beside the road, he told me to 'hop in'. He pointed out a field to the left and asked if 'it'd do fur de horses?' The field was huge, coated in heather with little grass, and the sea was close on three sides. It would be very exposed to bad weather, but a large steep hill in the centre of the field would provide shelter, whatever the wind direction. The lack of grazing wouldn't normally be a problem for Shetland ponies in winter – (it is, after all, this type of landscape that they evolved in), but a nursing mother and a young foal would need extra feed. I wondered about affordability of the field and winter feed, before deciding that I needed them here, and I would find a way to pay for it. I thanked Lowrie profusely, promising I would take good care of the fences. Although he never said or did anything to make me feel that the horses were unwelcome, my suspicions that he was letting me use the field out of kindness and against his better judgement were confirmed when, at a party, I heard several people say versions of: 'Horses! I saw horses in Lowrie's park. Nivver thought I would see the day.'

They arrived on a cold, damp day. A near gale, showers, and occasional gaps in the cloud combined to form fleeting, fast-moving rainbows that brightened the steel-grey sky. My heart sank as I saw the text alert from the ferries. The *Linga* had broken down, leading to delays and cancellations. I stood nervously by the water's edge watching waves crash over the bow of the *Filla*, the small replacement vessel, as she weaved her way towards the harbour. When I saw the unmistakable shape of a horsebox on board, relief washed over me. They were here.

I sat watching as the ponies calmly explored their surroundings. The view from the field was spectacular – ever changing, sea and sky shifting, responding to the day's weather. Cars passed on the narrow road below and a flock of sheep moved purposefully, finding shelter in the lee of a hill moments before a heavy rain shower. I had visited Yukon several times at Jackie's, spending time grooming her and hoping to build some trust so she felt safe in her new home. It seemed to have worked: Yukon approached me, curious and only a little hesitant, and put her nose right up to mine, then stood while I scratched her neck. I suddenly noticed she was still wearing her halter: I had to remove it before I left. Taking hold of the bottom of the halter, I accidentally pulled her beard. She reared, her tiny form suddenly high above me. Worried she might get hurt, I let go, and instantly regretted it. Yukon darted a few feet away. Her body was tense as she watched me, alert for any further move I might make. Each time I stepped towards her she edged away, staying close but not allowing me near enough to touch her. I started to panic – this was her first day and already I was getting everything wrong.

I knew the houses nearby would likely be watching events unfold, and that I would need to write a truthful account of the day's activities in my fieldnotes, so I was hyper-aware of every move she and I made. I could see only one solution: to get her into a corner where she couldn't get away. I enlisted Steve's help and we approached her from two sides, forcing her back towards the fence. When Yukon realised she was trapped, she stood, nostrils flaring, eyes wild, whinnying desperately to her mum who was watching closely. I worried what Sugar might do if she thought we were hurting her foal. Slowly, I placed the leadrope gently around Yukon's neck, speaking softly to her the whole time. Her ears twitched and her tiny body quivered, but she made no move to get away. Unfastening the halter, I let the rope slip off her. The second she was free she ran to her mum and together they raced over the hill, away from me, and I knew my clumsiness had broken the small amount of trust we had developed.

I felt joy as I visited them every day, walking up the road towards them, feed bucket in my hand, knowing they were there. Their presence provided companionship, a reassuring structure to my day and a feeling of becoming more connected to what I was writing about. Initially it was hard to find them in their large field – they didn't know when to expect me and I hadn't yet learned their favourite places. Whenever Sugar saw me approach, she would whinny and walk purposefully towards me, putting her head deep into the feed bucket as soon as I set it on the ground. Yukon still seemed wary of me after the halter incident, keeping her distance, always staying just out of reach. All the pony breeders I had met had emphasised the importance of not pressuring ponies into contact, saying it was best to just be there and let them come to you when they were ready. So I stroked and patted Sugar, holding my hand out to Yukon but not making any move towards her. Gradually, as the days passed, she began to approach, sniffing at my hand or bringing her face close to mine. In these moments, I stayed as still as I could, as the slightest move, shifting position, a cough, or even my hair or clothing blowing in the wind, would cause her to flee.

One morning, as soon as I entered the field she came over and stood beside me. I moved slowly, reaching out to scratch her rump. Although she kept a wary eye on me, she gradually moved closer, allowing me to scratch her neck and shoulders. (This would become a regular part of our time together, and as she grew more comfortable she'd start to 'groom' me back, running her teeth gently over my arms and shoulders.) Sugar, who had until this point mostly ignored me, coming for the food bucket but moving away soon after, came over to join us. I scratched her chest and she started to groom Yukon's withers. The wind was biting cold, the ground soaking and the sky threatened rain, but I had no urge to go back to the warm house. This field was where I now felt most at home.

Halter training

Now that I had a foal to train – a foal whose early experiences of halters, ropes and human contact would be shaped by her days with me – I thought a lot about what I had learned from Shetland breeders. One day in particular stood out: when I'd joined the Robin's Brae stud as they'd worked with their foals. Steve had filmed the process, and as I watched the footage I was transported back to that summer day.

The heavy rain in the early morning had cleared. The sun shone and a fresh breeze sent clouds racing across the sky, leaving intricate patterns of light and shade across the ground. Sounds of scuffling feet and high-pitched whinnies came from the stone byre as foals tried to communicate with their mums in the field outside. It was a busy day: foal microchipping, halter training and vet checks were all on the itinerary, leading to a near-constant coming and going of animals and people between the byre and the field.

Before we began Leona explained that the aim was to have foals do as she asked because they chose to, not because they were being forced. At the same time, she emphasised that foals must learn to behave in the ways that are expected of them. 'It's about mutual respect, but it is a battle of wills at the same time,' she said. They used a natural system of reward where the foal's nose was briefly cupped or stroked when they responded correctly. This method aimed to mimic natural interactions within a horse herd rather than introducing artificial rewards such as food.

The first foal she brought out was Toto, a miniature

black colt wearing a red halter. Leona pulled on Toto's rope, gently at first then with more force as he pulled back. She explained that the beginning is the hardest part because the foals don't understand what you want, and the new sensation of the halter can make them feel trapped. When Leona started to apply more pressure to the rope, Toto dug his heels into the ground, tossed his head, then pulled back in a sudden and violent motion. His tiny hoofs scrabbled clumsily against the ground as he tried to resist the increased pressure on the rope. As she pulled harder, he started to move forward in reluctant bursts of motion.

After a few steps, Leona stopped and Toto struggled and pulled back with all his strength. Leona held the rope firm, not pulling but not lessening her grip. After a few moments Toto began to struggle less. Leona pulled gently on the rope and Toto took a small step forward. Immediately, Leona loosened the tautness of the rope, stroked the foal's nose, and spoke softly to him. She turned to me and said, 'Every step they take towards you needs to be rewarded so they understand what you are asking them to do.' Toto started to pull again and Leona held tightly on to the rope. He pulled harder and harder, then threw himself down. As soon as he hit the ground he sprang back up, pulling frantically before rearing and throwing himself down once again. Leona spoke gently but kept tight hold of the rope. She explained, 'You canna loosen your grip. He'd think I was rewarding him and get confused.' Toto got to his feet, pulled a little, but then took another step forward and was instantly rewarded. The next fifteen minutes were a mixture of reward and resistance, but gradually his pulling back became less and his steps forward increased.

Now that he was moving forward more, after each step forward Leona would turn to the side and apply pressure to the rope, encouraging Toto to walk in circles around her. As he did this he started to chew. Leona said this was a sign she always paid attention to, as it meant they were starting to submit to you. She pointed: 'See how he is watching me more now – he is watching my every move and I am watching his.' As Leona walked, Toto began to follow more willingly, and before long he was taking steps towards her with only slight pressure on the rope. Amidst the sounds of *baa*-ing sheep and whinnying ponies, one horse's call became louder, shriller and more insistent. Toto's ears twitched and turned his head towards the byre in response to his mum's calls. Leona decided that it was a good time to end the day's lesson, before he became too tired and distracted. As we walked back to the byre, Leona said Toto had done a lot better than she'd expected. 'He was by our hoose an' is one of the tamest foals and they can be difficult to work with. You want them to be tame enough to work wi but not so tame that they dinna have respect fur you.'

Architectures of domestication

In traditional narratives about domestication, where domestication relationships are assumed to be based on control and subjugation of animals, tools such as ropes and halters are often described as the mechanisms through which humans force animals to do their bidding. While I was working with Sugar and Yukon, a paper published by colleagues in the Arctic Domus project, called 'Architectures of Domestication', sought to change the narrative on tools. They argued that tools need to be understood within their context: their meaning and purposes are defined by how they are understood and used as part of social life between species. As I worked with Shetland breeders, I saw how tools like halters were a key part of interspecies communication. Halter training wasn't simply a task where breeders tried to make foals act in a particular way by teaching them to follow commands. It was also an opportunity for breeder and foal to learn from and about each other. Whenever I was with people working on tasks like halter training, these days were filled with observations about temperament, personality and what sort of life may suit that foal. At Robin's Brae, Toto's known tameness had been expected to manifest in stubbornness when it came to following instruction, but the experience of working with him changed that assessment. He made himself, his personality and his intentions known through his interactions with halter and rope. This time together was a practice of ongoing communication.

Gradually, in the weeks that followed, as I spent time with Yukon, I began to direct my attention, focusing on the parts of her body that would need to be touched most in her life. My fingers would trace the lines where her halter would sit, and I'd run my hands down her legs and over her hoofs. As she eased into this routine, I slowly introduced the halter. Initially I just brought it along with me, placing it on the ground and letting her sniff and explore, before finally slipping the band over her nose. Curious and only a little hesitant, from the start she seemed eager to participate in halter training with me.

A few weeks into training, I sat with Yukon, scratching her neck, an action that usually resulted in her 'grooming' me back; but that day something seemed different. Her movements were jerkier, and when she groomed my arm, she kept pausing to look at me, and I got the distinct impression that she was planning something. I realised she was going to bite the second before she did it. But I stayed still, waiting to see what would happen. Sure enough, she administered a sharp nip to my arm. I raised my voice and used a stern tone – not too much, as it was the first time I had told her off, but still, she leaped backwards, her whole body tense as she watched me from a distance. I sat ignoring her and spoke to Sugar. Yukon started to creep towards me, slowly, pausing often. She stood beside me, chewing, a sign I had been taught to recognise as a submissive gesture. I waited a moment before speaking softly to her and resuming scratching her chest, and she immediately and enthusiastically started grooming my arm in return.

About a week later I was working on teaching her to walk alongside. Putting on her halter, I started to walk while simultaneously saying, 'Walk on.' She very quickly learned what was expected of her and willingly engaged. This day she appeared more resistant than usual, stopping regularly. When she did start walking I sensed she didn't want to, and that she was not enjoying the day's activity. I decided it would be best to cut this lesson short and work on something else. Then she stopped again, planted all four feet, and absolutely refused to move. Although I had been planning to stop, many breeders had warned against 'letting the horse win', and so I knew I had to get her started, walk her more, and then stop when it was clear that it was my instruction that was ending the lesson. So, with a pull of the rope and a push from behind, she was moving again, her body tense, her steps jerky, her head moving more than usual, and suddenly I knew she was going to nip. As she turned her head towards me, I gave a sharp tug to the rope and said, 'No,' in a stern tone. She moved her head away, began chewing, then continued walking. I took her in several large circles before I said it was time to stop, and not once in that time did she show any signs of stopping or trying to bite.

This is a moment that I have thought about a lot. I reprimanded her before she did anything. Because I thought she was going to bite. But why did I think that? And was she going to do it? I am still sure she was, but I am most interested in how I came to that conclusion. Moving her head towards me while walking alongside was something she did often – sometimes to look at me, sometimes for a quick sniff or a nuzzle – so why did it feel so different that time? I had sensed she was in a bad mood from the start of the day, before I'd even put the halter on. I thought back: what were the signs I was picking up on? I thought about the signals people had told me to look out for but I didn't think any of those really applied. There was maybe a little more tension in her body but no specific identifiable signal that I could be sure of, or that I could easily describe to others. This sense of knowing what she was going to do and the difficulty explaining how I came to that conclusion reminded me of what breeders described about 'just knowing' what their ponies were thinking. I wondered if this was my first tangible experience of this with Yukon.

Although knowing their ponies, and respecting equine ideas and opinions, was central to the practice of pony breeders across Shetland, how they came to their conclusions was something I initially had trouble understanding. As people told me details about ponies' personalities, attitudes or moods, I would ask them how they knew. One of my main PhD research questions focused on how people got to know and understand their animals, and I was desperate to learn how the complex relationships of mutual respect and understanding developed in practice. How did people get to know their ponies' opinions? But whenever I asked these questions, I got fairly standard answers such as, 'When their ears are back it shows they are in a bad mood.' I found this very frustrating: these types of explanations are very simplistic cause-and-effect readings of animal behaviour that you would find in any horse care manual. It was clear to me that the process of getting to know ponies' personalities required a far deeper level of understanding of pony communication, but one that people found hard to put into words.

When people did start to describe 'just knowing' what ponies were feeling, or being able to 'read their minds', they would pause, looking at me to check my reaction. If they continued, they would often add qualifiers like, 'You will probably think me mad,' or, 'Maybe I just imagine this but I feel it's true.' I was surprised that these people, who had such respect for the individuality and intelligence of their animals, should hesitate to such an extent when describing how they'd learned such things. As I thought about it, however, I realised we often don't have the language to adequately discuss cross-species communication.

Robin Wall Kimmerer, in her beautiful book *Braiding Sweetgrass*, describes the limitations of English for describing the world. It is a language with more nouns than verbs, named things rather than living beings. By considering a non-human as 'it' rather than 'who', we create and maintain a separation, ignoring or failing to notice the animacy of the worlds we inhabit. These ideas of separations, between humans, animals and landscapes, are reinforced by mainstream and scientific discussions. Too often, any statement that claims to understand the feelings, motivations or intentions of an animal, or even the idea that animals have these kinds of mental capabilities, is seen as anthropomorphic. Humans are thought to project their own ideas onto animals, attributing human-like emotions to them.

This implies that we don't think animals are capable of such experiences and emotions, assuming from the outset that there are certain characteristics that are unique to humans. If we describe a dog's sadness or a horse's empathy as anthropomorphic, then we are claiming that these are human emotions that we are extending, fictitiously, to the animals in our lives. Even if we believe that such emotions are present, they are thought to be inaccessible to members of different species. In much of Western psychology, thoughts and intentions are understood as abstract representations contained inside a mind that may then be acted upon by the individual. The only way to understand this inner state would be through somehow experiencing the world as others do, something thought to be impossible in human–animal relationships.

Recently in human–animal studies there have been moves towards understanding thoughts as being in the world rather than contained inside individuals. Thoughts and motivations are not inaccessible, locked away within individual minds, but rather they can be understood as part of unfolding relationships. Vinciane Despret describes this as 'with-ness', where through time and attention, participants in a relationship together develop new understandings of the worlds they share. For the breeders I worked with, the fact that ponies were equines – members of a different species – was not thought to be an impenetrable barrier to communication or understanding. Through their shared lives, people became attuned to their ponies. Equine opinions and preferences emerged through embodied attention, how ponies lived with weather and land, and how they responded to the tools of domestication: halters, ropes and hands.

Getting to know ponies, taking time to understand and communicate with them, was central to how people understood their own identities as responsible pony breeders. As they sought to breed true island-type ponies and maintain relationships between ponies, people and place, effective communication was central to this. Halter training and learning to communicate with ponies was an important part of ensuring a good future for individual ponies, but it was also a fundamental way of imagining futures for the breed.

Futures

One morning, as I sat with Yukon, I suddenly remembered the foals at the sale, the ones nobody had wanted, sold for less than the price of a takeaway coffee. What had become of them? I wondered what Yukon's life would be: if she would stay in Shetland or find home somewhere new; if she might become a broodmare or a child's pony. I traced my fingers along her body. Her proportions were correct, she was pretty and clearly intelligent, but it was likely she would grow to be the unpopular mid-size, and I worried this could reduce her options. I knew that using the halter with her was opening up communication, a shared understanding, but I hoped it was doing more, that I was also helping increase her future chances.

People and ponies live in a shared world, each responding to the other, so ponies need to learn to live and belong as part of the rhythms of human lives. Halter training is a time to establish effective and respectful communication. Although not wanting to dominate or over-domesticate their ponies, breeders also believe too much freedom, or freedom at the wrong time, could be detrimental to the lives of their horses. Training involves an intricate balance of communication and coercion, autonomy and control, as breeders use their skills to increase the future options for their ponies. Several breeders described times where they'd inadvertently 'made a fool' of a pony by allowing a foal to become too tame, being too lax with halter training, or encouraging silly behaviours. This resulted in adult horses who would rush up to people and try to sit on their knee, engaged in attention-seeking behaviours and were less able to appropriately engage in essential tasks such as hoof trimming. Breeders saw teaching foals how to live as part of human social worlds as an important part of their job, often comparing it to the role of parents teaching younger generations what behaviour is expected. Training a pony correctly was thus to equip them with the skills necessary to share their lives with humans and ensure the possibility of meaningful communication.

On the other hand, too much human control was also thought to be bad for relationships, robbing ponies of their autonomy. Lots of breeders worried about how tightly controlled the lives of many horses were, leaving little room for the horse to experience freedom or learn to think for themselves. Over time, horses may lose their natural instincts, becoming increasingly dependent on human care. One day when I bumped into Roselyn on the ferry, we chatted about Yukon and I asked her how Hirta was doing with her training. She said Hirta had learned a lot over summer and was clearly enjoying ridden work, but that now it was time for her to have a break. 'She is going back to June for the winter, to spend some time on the hill,' Roselyn explained. 'Once they have learned, they need time to think, to process. If they get worked all the time then they forget to think for themselves. It is like they end up on autopilot.'

With too much domination comes the possibility of a breakdown in communication between species, as humans forget how to listen to horses. Within such relationships, where horses' voices are ignored, they may stop speaking to us over time, the shared language becoming forgotten. The breeders I met in Shetland prioritised time with their ponies, time to learn with and from them, reading each other's language and establishing the boundaries of their shared worlds.

There are elements of hierarchy present when breeders work with tools. Some tasks are not optional, but I don't believe this contradicts assertions of respecting equine autonomy. Relationships and the tools that are part of them are complex, multifaceted, shifting with the social contexts they are part of. It is precisely the recognition of ponies as intelligent companions who should be listened to that makes halter training so important.

Winter

In Shetland folklore, each spring the Sea Mither battles Teran, the bringer of storms, forcing him to the depth of the ocean so the islands can enjoy the peace of good weather. As autumn approaches, however, the Sea Mither grows tired, and Teran, taking advantage of her weakness, fights again for control over the sea.

October was filled with the evidence of these battles. Strong winds appeared from nowhere, raising the sea into a fury of swell and spray, storms that could last anything from a few hours to several days. The silence of the times in between felt absolute: sun, still air and the absence of seabirds. The grass on the ness remained green but brown was returning to the hills, and the wildflowers that had coloured the summer had retreated until spring. Although the sun kept some of its warmth, it stayed lower to the horizon, shadows stretching long across the landscape as evening encroached earlier into each day. By the end of the month the feel of the wind had changed, carrying stories of distant snow as it swept across the island.

The changing season had a profound effect on Yoda. Although he would still wait at the gate for food, once he had eaten he would rejoin the flock as they returned to the hill. Throughout the day he followed them, moving with them as they grazed, his body language mirroring theirs. From a distance, he was indistinguishable from the rest of the flock.

'It's the time that rams to go to the yowes,' Lowrie explained. 'He must sense it. He will stay with them now he knows how.' I watched as he and Four White Feet stood grooming each other. My little orphan lamb had finally found his sheep family. A few days later I saw a post on Facebook from June, saying that all her ponies had been down at the gate waiting to be fed for the first time that year. Below were many comments from other breeders saying that it was the same for their ponies, that this was the day they'd asked for food. Later June told me that every year this always amazes her, how ponies miles apart in different parts of Shetland all at the same time sensed the same change in season, and knew how to tell their humans.

Despite the darkening days as winter approached, my days felt lighter. Sitting outside in this wild landscape with a tiny foal, a new member of an ancient breed, I felt a growing sense of excitement about my research and renewed hope for the future. As the weeks were progressing Yukon's foal fuzz was growing, transforming into the thick winter coat that would protect her from the elements. She stood, pressing her nose against mine, our breath visible in the chill of the air, merging in a cloud that surrounded us, before travelling with the wind, away from this small corner that I now called home.

9

CHRISTMAS

DECEMBER BROUGHT STORMS, WEEKS OF gales and lashing rain, the leaden skies darkening the already-limited daylight hours. As I looked at the weather forecast, the wind speed seemed to always be marked in red or orange: gale force 8, severe gale force 9 or storm force 10. I tried to avoid travelling on days where the forecast was bad, fearing ferry cancellations that would leave me stranded, but with no change in the weather predicted, I still needed to travel to the mainland for fieldwork. I always visited the ponies before catching the morning ferry, my torch beam highlighting the rain, making visible the force of the wind. I usually knew where in the field they would be, learning the places that offered shelter from various weather conditions. As I gave them their food they would stand, rain dripping from their coats, bums to the wind, weathering the storms.

Rain and waves would bounce off my windscreen as the ferry was tossed from side to side, reigniting my old fear of the car sliding helplessly off the boat into the dark water. The winter somehow made me feel more aware of being on a small island, part of an archipelago, miles from the nearest land. Driving off the ferry at night and leaving behind the few streetlights in Symbister meant driving into absolute darkness. The lights of small groups of houses had once seemed to emphasise the landscape's emptiness, yet now I understood how these houses were connected as part of vast networks of community. When island homes had their porch lights on it indicated that visits were welcome, and as I passed, I thought of the social worlds these lights indicated. I loved this feeling of islandness, of warmth and safety, surrounded by the elements.

Christmas lights started to appear in December, transforming familiar houses. Coloured lights traced the outlines of buildings, surrounded window frames, sheds and fences. Bright, glowing snowmen and reindeer arrived in gardens, and boats in the harbour kept the lights on their masts lit. Robbie and Ina invited us round for Christmas dinner. I was really touched by this gesture, and a little relieved. Watching families preparing for the festive season, I had felt quite lonely at the thought of just me and Steve together on Christmas Day. Seeing the evidence of islanders' connections, to family and community, heightened my sense that I had never had such networks of belonging. Although the miscarriage had meant an end to the pregnancy nausea, the sadness I felt during autumn meant it took some time for me to re-engage, slowly beginning to take part in local activities again.

Although I was coming to terms with my miscarriage, events like Christmas, when I would have been entering my third trimester, getting ready to welcome the baby, suddenly felt particularly lonely, the sense of loss more palpable.

The weather eased on Christmas Eve, so I decided to venture to the mainland to pick up a few extra supplies. I heard the Coastguard helicopter in the distance, and to my surprise it flew directly towards the centre of town, getting lower and lower until it was barely above the houses. I could see people shouting and waving and I worried someone was experiencing an emergency, until I realised the children were shouting, 'Santa! Santa!' Sure enough, Santa Claus was leaning out of the helicopter door, waving. The helicopter flew in several large circles over the town before continuing north. I was told later that was a Shetland Christmas Eve tradition, and every year Rescue 900 carries Santa and his elf all over Shetland.

I realised I had several hours before my ferry booking, and not wanting to take my chances in the unbooked queue, I decided to take a trip to the Stanydale Temple. The temple dates back to the Neolithic and is the only structure of its size and kind in Shetland. Like most of the island's ancient sites, it is without fences and is open to all.

I have always loved visiting places of ritual and magic at special times of year – solstices, equinoxes, Beltane, the times where the boundaries between worlds feel at their most porous. The sun was just above the horizon, casting long beams of golden light across the ancient stones, set in a circle, revealing the presence of lives lived here before. A flock of sheep, their fleeces backlit, appeared to glow as they made their way across the hill. The silent air was suddenly filled with the voices and wingbeats of five swans flying west, towards the sea. The presence of swans and stone reminded me of the words of my favourite poem, 'Swans at Brodgar' by George Mackay Brown:

Circles compel us everywhere,
Sun and stone and bird-flight.
Ancient wisdom knew the law of circles,
Instructing the quarrymen and masons of Brodgar
In the purity and inevitability of stone-setting.

And the great white birds,
Caught in a random circle of repose
Will rise again to the blood's curve and thrust.

I stood by the entrance stones, where the first rays of the solstice sunrise still line up exactly with the doorway. I thought about the farmers, living 5,000 years ago, in this landscape, and how dark the midwinter must have seemed to them. The disconnect between my life, hopes and worries and theirs seemed vast. Yet the seasons, cycles of time, and the importance of special places continue, albeit in an altered form. I had been in Shetland for nearly a year, experiencing the full circle of seasons, feeling myself changing in more ways than I had expected when I began my journey north. In this place, in silence, surrounded by the presence of time, I felt at peace, ready for whatever the new year would bring. I took a small shell from my pocket and laid it beside one of the stones An offering? A gesture of thanks? I didn't know, but it somehow felt like the right thing to do.

Over Christmas dinner people shared stories about life on the island, the people, animals and memorable events. Many of the people and places were now familiar to me, and I felt as though these stories were weaving us, slowly, into the community. As evening drew in, Steve and I headed home, discussing what we should do now. When we had spoken about our Christmas plans with our neighbours, they had said, 'Joost come by ony time,' but suddenly I had doubts – had they really meant on Christmas Day? Would we be intruding if we turned up? Or perhaps we were being rude and separating ourselves from the community if we didn't? I began over thinking it, getting myself into a nervous fluster, until we decided just to go over and wish everyone a merry Christmas and see where things went. As soon as the door opened we were warmly welcomed into the house with a 'Sit de doon,' as glasses were placed in our hands and drinks poured.

Different parts of Whalsay have different traditions around Christmas. Some have island-wide parties in public halls, while others are local affairs, where most of the people taking part live in or have a close connection to one of the surrounding townships. The north of the island, where we lived, had a large bonfire on Boxing Day. That night, the wind carried the feel of frost and the thousands of stars above us seemed somehow brighter and closer as we met our neighbours at the road end. Several of the men held huge flaming torches, the same type the guizers carry during winter Up Helly Aa fire festivals. Together we walked down the road towards the glowing light in the valley below. The fire was roaring, its welcome warmth spreading through the cold night air. A variety of furniture – sofas, tables, bookshelves, lamps and even a TV – had been placed around the fire. Some people were settled on this furniture, while others stood around in small groups chatting, and some teenagers gathered at the top of a peat bank. People came with their whisky bottles, offering everybody a sip in turn. The atmosphere was warm and welcoming, everybody full of laughter.

As the fire reduced to embers, people started to move inside, with calls for the crowd to follow and join the party. Inside the warm house, homemade soup, bannocks and island-smoked fish were laid out in the kitchen. We took some food, accepted a dram, and made our way to the living room, struggling to find somewhere to sit in the crowded room. As folk talked and laughed there was an element of parody and pantomime, something that was becoming a familiar part of Shetland social life. Throughout Shetland culture, there is a strong desire to not appear boastful. Even experts in their field, with undeniable skills and experience, are likely to play down their expertise, to stress that they know 'only a little', and often emphasise the role of others in their achievements. Related to this is a strong distrust towards those who profess to know about something they have little experience of, and a dislike of people who take themselves too seriously. Those associated with such 'hot air' were often ridiculed and parodied at parties and social gatherings, and this night was no exception. Through 'speeches', conversations and pantomime, well-known Shetland people and institutions were gently, but pointedly, mocked. I didn't understand all the references, but when I did I laughed along with the group, feeling happy and included.

Every party we attended was relaxed, vibrant and welcoming. Glasses were refilled at an alarming rate, and usually I would have several drinks lined up in front of me as I failed to keep up with the pace. Despite enjoying these events, I felt I needed a little more time to recover from socialising than my island neighbours, and by the time Newardy arrived, I was exhausted. The largest celebration for New Year is the night of 1 January, rather than 31 December as is traditional in Scotland. That evening, the township of five houses where we lived was open house to the whole island. From dusk until dawn, people arrived to have a drink and pass on good wishes for the coming year. I sat in neighbours' houses, mesmerised by the constant flow of guests, each sitting for some time, accepting a dram, sharing stories and jokes, before moving along to the next house. Later, as I lay in bed, I could hear the parties continuing, each new visitor met with enthusiastic greetings, and those leaving having well wishes shouted after them. I smiled as I thought how different this was from city celebrations, where entry into people's homes requires invites and is often limited to close friends and family. I felt so happy and grateful to live in such a sociable place, where speaking to those who lived near you was not just possible but expected. I loved the freedom and flexibility of island socialising, even though I was still unsure how to properly participate. But despite the amount of time I spent off the island for fieldwork and my lack of community participation due to illness, I was still welcomed by my neighbours. I was invited to parties and celebrations, included in the sharing of fish and eggs, and I really felt I was beginning to belong, that this was where I needed to be. As I drifted off to sleep, I vowed to start the new year with a renewed effort to be part of the community that I was growing to love.

A new year

I could hardly bear to look at the photograph but felt drawn to it, like a compulsion. Retrieving it from the drawer, I stared at the grainy black-and-white image, a frozen moment, capturing a tiny heartbeat, the start of life, made visible by technology. I had been lucky: the molar clinic had quickly given me the all clear so we had been free to try for another baby. Before long, a pregnancy test had shown that longed-for second line.

The weather that week was beautiful, warm with little wind. These days were rare, and as soon as they arrived, everybody made the most of them. Folk spent longer on outdoor tasks, chatting to friends and neighbours as they repaired storm damage, worked with their animals, or prepared gardens for spring planting. The small main road around the island became filled with people walking. I felt full of hope as I chatted to friends and neighbours and spent time with the ponies. The molar pregnancy had just been bad luck, I told myself. This time would be different.

My elation quickly turned to fear when, as I walked up the hill to see Yukon, I realised I was bleeding. I went home and, in floods of tears, called the maternity department. The midwife I spoke to was kind but said that as I had only just had a scan we would need to wait a few days before scanning again to see if this pregnancy was progressing, or if it too had failed. I didn't know what to do with myself during this wait. I spent hours on the internet, trying to find hope from stories of bleeds where the pregnancy was fine, but found myself drawn towards all the possible negative outcomes: miscarriage, ectopic pregnancy, or perhaps another molar. The spell of fine weather continued, but when I saw people outside chatting I felt unable to join in, weighed down by my worries. Instead I sat high above the road in Yukon's field, separate, watching the world go by.

When I next entered the scan room I was shaking, my legs moving mechanically, unable to find the words to respond to the midwife's friendly greetings. As soon as the scanner touched my stomach, the midwife turned the screen towards me, a fluttering heartbeat, clearly visible. My relief was short-lived, however, as a matter of hours after that scan I was bleeding again. Huge clots, a heavier period than I had ever known. I arrived back at the door of maternity in tears, panicking, sure the life I had just seen was gone. Again, within seconds, the screen was turned, the tiny heart still beating. Due to the extent of the blood loss, I was admitted to the ward, where I spent the night awake, listening to the cries of a newborn in the next room, wondering if my baby was still OK. After a quick scan the next morning I was discharged with a warning that these bleeds may recur, and to come back immediately if it happened again. The midwife was kind and supportive, advising that it would be hard, but to take each day as it came. That time might seem to stand still, but it would still move, and this time would pass.

It took days for it to really sink in that I was still pregnant. It felt so uncertain, tenuous, all the time wondering if that little heart inside me was still beating. Normal life became too much. The fear of bleeding stayed with me. I could clearly remember the feeling the moment I realised what was happening, my chest tightening each time with the memory. I was terrified it would happen again, constantly going to the bathroom to make sure there was no blood. I have always worried more than most people, imagining scenarios many steps away from my current situation. I'd generally understood this as being part of me, existing alongside, and probably directly related to, my rather active imagination. Over the years I had found ways to manage many aspects of my anxiety, preventing it from becoming a determining influence on my life. Life in Shetland had helped me recognise and address other patterns of anxious thinking that had, over the years, grown to become a bigger part of me than I had realised.

Yet now, for the first time, I felt anxiety taking over. I became overwhelmed at the thought of going anywhere. What would I do if I was out in a field with a pony breeder and started bleeding? I knew what the sensible answer was, but I couldn't handle the thought of making my apologies and driving to the hospital. I decided that I would take it easy for a few weeks, but even the most mundane tasks became difficult. Halfway around Tesco, trolley full of shopping, I was convinced I had started bleeding. I froze. I didn't know what to do. Should I just leave the trolley and rush to the loo or continue with the shopping? I picked up a few more items and joined the nearest queue. Panic washed over me in waves, my face wet with cold sweat. I felt exposed, like everybody could see my fear, wondering why I was acting so oddly. I concentrated on breathing and focused on placing the items, one at a time, onto the conveyer belt. As soon as I had paid, trying hard to make the correct small talk with the cashier, I raced to the toilet, where I found there was no blood. I sank down onto the seat, my legs like jelly, weeping uncontrollably.

Animal therapy

Winter was starting to recede, and the now-familiar signs of spring returned. The oystercatchers' shrill cries, fulmars forming pairs and settling into their homes in broken-down walls, the bubbling call of curlew. Out on the water, rafts of eider ducks floated past, black and white and brown shapes, their surprised 'oooohh-hhs' always making me smile, pulling me away from my worries, if only for a moment. The remains of small blue eggshells told me that the first broods of starling chicks had arrived, and before long, as soon as I stepped near a stone wall, the clamour of hungry babies in the nest would explode from between the stones. As I walked along the ness, I often stopped to sit on a rock and look out to sea. Seeing me, Yoda always left his flock, and raced down to stand next to me, grazing inches from my feet. When I reached out to scratch his cheeks or neck, he would put his head to one side, often resting it on my knee, and close his eyes as he peacefully chewed the cud.

There were several days of bright, dry weather, where the sun shone and there was only a light breeze. After a long winter, I loved the feeling of being surrounded by the feel of spring, yet there was a disconnect. The warmth and stillness seemed at odds with my racing thoughts and frantic worries. I don't know how I would have got through those difficult months if it hadn't been for the presence of the ponies. I am sure Yukon knew something was different. In the weeks before I had become pregnant she had not spent much time close to me. She had been working well on the halter, seeming to enjoy walks along the road, barely paying any notice to her mum's frantic whinnies as I led her out of the field. As soon as we returned, and I took the halter off, she would take off, full-speed, playfully running around, bucking and generally showing off. But the day of the first bleed, as I'd sat in her field, in a terrible limbo, she'd come straight up to me, quietly, her body touching mine, and had stood close. As I'd cried, she had pressed her face up to mine. Alongside the worry, my clearest memory of that day is the feel of her coat and her warm breath on my face, as the world continued around us, and we were still.

With the changing season Sugar and Yukon started to lose their winter coats. They stood with eyes half closed and bottom lips drooping as I brushed them. More hair than I imagined possible came out with every stroke. Sugar rested her head on my shoulder, her chestnut coat glowing like fire in the sunlight. Yukon stood beside us, gently grooming her mum's flanks. My days were filled with the rhythmic sounds of brush strokes, as I sat watching tufts of hair travel slowly across the field in the light breeze, before being carried away by opportunistic starlings who recognised good-quality nesting material. I know that one of the reasons the horses stayed with me for hours at a time was because they were itchy and the grooming I gave them helped relieve the discomfort, but it was more than that. They were more present, patient and affectionate, and though I am sure they didn't understand my words, I have no doubt they knew something was wrong and were trying to help. The way they were during those weeks was so different than at any other time. I needed to be close to them, taking comfort from the warmth and strength of their bodies.

Many people shared similar experiences with me, and my notebooks were filled with stories of the deep, healing bonds between people and ponies. Brenda, a young woman who now lives on the Scottish mainland, described how she spent her childhood out in the field or hill, surrounded by ponies. One mare in particular was her constant companion. She described how one day, after receiving difficult news, she'd gone out to the hill and this mare had put her head on her shoulder, giving her a cuddle when she'd needed it most. Now she lived in a city and was increasingly struggling with the lack of animal connections in her life. She described the loneliness of no longer having the option to walk into the hill, to be with ponies, when things were difficult. She kept pictures of her ponies on her wall and tried to visit Shetland regularly to maintain the connections, but she said her separation from the place she'd grown up, and the ponies that remained there, was something she found more difficult with each year that passed.

Perhaps one of the most memorable stories was one June told me. A father and daughter had visited her stud. The young girl was blind and June had been concerned that the foals, who spent most of their time excitedly chasing each other round the field, might be a little too rambunctious with the girl. When they'd arrived at the field all the horses had come over to them. Very gently, the mares and the foals had brought their heads close to the girl, allowing her to stroke them. After some time the mares had walked away and had started grazing, but the foals had stayed with the girl and had walked with her to the gate. June said she had never known the foals to ever act this way, and that they had just known, without anyone having to tell them, what the girl had needed.

At Burland Croft, Mary had introduced me to the ponies she kept close by for visitors to meet. She had a box of brushes in the field for people to have a chance to groom the horses, and as we talked I would brush the ponies who had gathered around us. These were the ponies that Mary trusted 100 per cent – ones that she knew would stand patiently, even if children were clumsy and loud in their interactions with them. She would often watch as she went about the summer croft work, and described how children just 'lit up' when they were with ponies. Both Mary and her husband Tommy worried about how much time some children spent indoors these days, with some never having the chance to experience such first-hand contact with animals. They told me stories about several young people who had visited the croft over the years, some with additional support needs and others suffering from difficulties at home. From the first encounter, interactions with land and animals profoundly affected the children. Mary explained that these connections are natural, formed through centuries of children and Shetland ponies living together. Historically, in Shetland it was often children who worked with croft ponies, training foals, working the peat, and Shetland ponies were often a child's first riding pony. She said that the history of such relationships has shaped Shetland ponies today, so many of them instinctively 'just know' how to be with children. They are born with the capacity to understand and respond to the diverse needs and personalities of the children they meet.

As I sat with Sugar and Yukon, I remembered feeling lonely and scared as a child, and how I had found such comfort being with horses. How communication and shared understanding had felt so easy, so natural, at a time when little in the rest of my life had made sense. Now, decades later, when my mind was overflowing with worries, it was here, in the pony field, where I felt most at peace. I thought about the stories islanders had shared with me, about love and connection, shared experiences between species, and how when people describe keeping the true island-type characteristics in Shetland ponies – referring to physical strength, intelligence and adaptability – they are also seeking to protect more intangible qualities such as empathy and belonging. These skills were an important element of shared lives and could potentially open up new futures for the breed in therapy work. Some ponies from Shetland have already been sold to riding centres that specialise in providing support to people with additional needs. Their ability to respond to human emotion is something that has flowed through experience, rather than something ponies were actively taught or trained to do by their owners. It has developed over centuries with each generation, human and equine, teaching the next how to live well together in this place.

Flourishing landscapes

As I wrote my thesis, I noticed the theme of stories recurring throughout the chapters. I particularly loved these lines written by Anna Lowenhaupt Tsing:

> Over the past few decades, many kinds of scholars have shown that allowing only human protagonists into our stories is not just ordinary human bias; it is a cultural agenda tied to dreams of progress through modernization. There are other ways of making worlds. Anthropologists have become interested, for example,

in how subsistence hunters recognize other living beings as 'persons', that is, protagonists of stories. Indeed, how could it be otherwise? Yet expectations of progress block this insight: talking animals are for children and primitives. Their voices silent, we imagine well-being without them. We trample over them for our advancement; we forget that collaborative survival requires cross-species coordinations. To enlarge what is possible, we need other kinds of stories – including adventures of landscapes.

Stories are part of the fabric that makes our world; they are generative, shaping our world and what futures are possible. And so the stories we tell about domestication, how humans and animals live together, matter. Historically, much of Western-based knowledge systems – religion, science, philosophy – are predicated on a separation of humans and nature. Plants and animals are understood in rather mechanical ways, governed by innate biology and responding to stimuli, rather than as sentient beings capable of engaging in meaningful relationships. It is from within this context that the traditional narratives about domestication, which I have sought to challenge, emerged. Stories of humans as controlling animal lives, either celebrated as civilisation's achievement or lamented as the widespread enslavement of non-humans. Domination and violence don't have to be part of domestication relationships, but too often they are, and narratives that imply this is an inevitable part of domestication can legitimise, and naturalise, these exploitative practices. But when we tell other stories about our lives with domestic animals – stories of love and connection – these stories become part of our journey with non-humans, and can shape our shared worlds.

One line in particular from Tsing's quote really stood out to me: 'we imagine well-being without them'. We have told stories of human exceptionalism, of our separation from animals and landscapes, for so long that many of these connections are becoming forgotten. In the UK (as is the case in many countries around the world), lives are becoming more urbanised and technology-focused. Fewer adults or children spend time in rural landscapes or have the opportunity to interact with animals as part of their everyday lives. Even when people live in rural areas, changes to farming practices mean that there are fewer opportunities to interact with domestic animals. These separations, connected to and sometimes forced by particular economic and ideological systems, work to make us feel isolated from worlds we are inevitably part of. This encourages us to ignore the possibility of more-than-human interactions, and fail to notice the ways these worlds affect us, which closes down possibilities for future connections. If our identities are shaped through our relationships with others, what does this mean for humans? Are we suffering without understanding what we are missing, cut off from networks of relating that we depend upon? And how can we re-engage in ways that cultivate the possibility of mutual flourishing?

I thought about my journey to Shetland. My childhood was filled with animals and landscapes, their lives and stories as real and vibrant – perhaps even more so – that I found in worlds that were exclusively human, and I often felt most at home in the wild places I found. My teenage years were filled with adventures with horses, sea swimming and backpacking. My eventual separation from this was not deliberate; it just slowly happened that jobs and money tied me to the city, in a life where I felt perhaps not unhappy, but somehow less me. I hadn't known what I was looking for in Shetland; I had just known that something was missing. Looking back on my previous life, I wondered if I had perhaps become 'over-domesticated', like the Shetland ponies who had lost their connections to place.

Being surrounded by sea and weather, learning about and becoming part of a landscape and community where humans and animals lived together, felt more right than I could have imagined. Somehow, through the noise and busyness of city life, I had still known to listen and respond to a call, a yearning, that I hadn't quite understood. Spending my days with ponies and the people who loved them, I had learned about myself and the types of world that it is possible to inhabit. As I worked with Arctic Domus colleagues to rethink and reimagine domestication, I felt renewed hope about the types of lives we can live with animals, and what this might mean for sustainable futures.

I learned that domination was not the founding principle of these domestication relationships. It was *domus* meaning 'home': a home shared with animals, a home comprising myriad meaningful interspecies relationships. This history of shared lives and hopes for positive futures emerged from relationships in time and place, and I came to understand that domestication is an ongoing, changing relationship between people and ponies in Shetland. Each live and become with the other, and these relationships matter, shaping ideas of home and belonging. I heard stories, sometimes going back several generations, of the joy that spending time with ponies could bring. Pony breeders would often describe interactions with their animals as therapeutic, recounting incidents where ponies had been an important part of coping with difficult circumstances. I believe, however, the contribution of ponies to health and well-being goes far beyond these memorable encounters. The experience of everyday living with ponies brings people joy. It is a practice of engaging with communities, human and non-human, while connecting to wider ideas about island histories.

When people work Shetland crofts, spending time with native breeds – cattle, sheep and ponies – they do so with attention towards the generations that came before and those who will come after. People notice the rhythms of their animals' lives, learning from them and with them. These embodied skills – how to pay attention, how to listen to horses – are an ongoing, engaged practice. To overly dominate or control the lives of Shetland breeds could inadvertently harm future relationships. Change has always been part of island life, and with uncertainty over trade and agriculture due to Brexit and a changing climate, people want to ensure that people and animals can adapt to whatever will come. Maintaining and adapting traditional skills is a way of keeping a degree of independence in Shetland, ensuring the possibility of liveable, sustainable landscapes into the future.

Through my time in Shetland, I began to understand domestication as a practice of cultivating a sense of home and belonging in the islands. Home stretched beyond the walls of the house, into the surrounding landscapes where animals lived. To be at home in this way is to be part of a living, sentient and connected landscape, feeling the way of the wind, being open to more than human communication. This is a home co-created through domestication relationships. These connections stretched through time, keeping alive the stories of the islands past, connecting them to present-day activities and actively creating and maintaining a valued way of life into the future. Each day's activities – grooming, feeding, showing – do not happen in isolation; they are part of vast communities, between generations of humans and animals, past, present and future. Working in this way, feeling a part of the place, actively contributing to the continuation of a distinct way of life, brings joy and a sense of purpose to people's lives. When writing my thesis, I often used the term 'liveable' in relation to these ideas: liveable landscapes for people and ponies. In my conclusion I made a typo: 'liveable' became 'loveable', but I realised that this is exactly what they are. Landscapes of love. Love of Shetland, its wild, rugged landscapes of barren hill surrounded by windswept coast. Love for the history, of independence despite exploitation, and survival against the odds. And of course, love for the animals, who allowed this survival and who continue to connect people to land and history.

The dancing sky

One night in March, just as I was going to go to bed, Robbie came to the door, telling me I should go out as there was a good show of aurora. Outside the air was cold and still. I walked along the ness, away from the lights of Vevoe, my eyes fixed on the curtains of green light glowing above the sea. They were in continual motion, and I immediately understood their Shetland name: Mirrie Dancers, where 'mirr' means 'blur'. This light was exactly like dancers moving across the sky, the speed of their movement obscuring their edges, as they merged with the darkness. The silvery-green shimmer was interspersed with pulses of orange and red light, moving along the horizon, reflected by the sea. And as I watched, I was sure I could hear them as they danced, a crackling hiss that filled the air. A more earthly sound joined it: the squelching of many hoofs in the mud, as Yoda, closely followed by his flock, appeared from over the hill. As I sat, surrounded by aurora and stars, with Yoda beside me, I felt transported by the magic of the moment. The anxiety that had been weighing me down lifted a little, and I felt sure that my upcoming scan would be fine, that there was new life inside me, and a beautiful world to introduce them to.

I began this book by sharing a moment walking to Sugar and Yukon, when I felt the intensity of connection between my actions and those of others who had come before. Although I often walked along that road to the ponies' field, there was something that morning, where I felt footsteps join theirs, separated only by time. Despite not having a history in Shetland, I had begun to feel part of the living world of this land. I had learned the power of generations of lives lived here, how these enduring connections bring joy and a sense of belonging. But I had also begun to understand how home is also a process, how being in a place, sharing our lives with others who live there, makes us who we are. As I thought about my growing baby, and the life I could give them, I vowed not to lament the connections that I didn't have, learning instead to make ones that matter, living in a way where I could feel the wind, and its stories of land and sea. I might not become permanently rooted here – or any place – but I felt more aware of how connections were made, more open to the stories of places, allowing these to become part of my and my new family's story.

EPILOGUE

TEARS STREAMED DOWN MY FACE as I sat among a sea of boxes holding a tiny white cardigan with blue buttons that Lowrie's wife, Anna, had knitted for my baby. This type of gift was one that would usually be brought in the days following birth, as islanders welcomed the new member of the community. Instead I was packing it in a box, as I was leaving Whalsay. My PhD didn't have a maternity provision; I could take time off sick, but there would be no extension to my funding. Due to PhD income not being counted as employment, I was also ineligible for any government maternity pay. This meant just a few months after giving birth my income would stop completely. We were moving to the island of Burra. As it is connected to Shetland mainland by a bridge, travel was more flexible, greatly increasing our employment options. But it felt so wrong to have to leave, when I was beginning to feel part of this community. There were several young children around Vevoe, and I knew our child would have been welcomed, would have had bonds of friendship and community from his very first day, and here I was severing these connections before they had a chance to form. I thought of all my clumsy attempts to be part of the community, how inadequate I had felt, and realised that I had still been accepted, included, and had begun to feel truly at home.

As the day to leave approached, my walks on the ness took on a new melancholy. I saw Yoda every day. Sometimes he remained with his flock and watched from a distance. Other days he bounded towards me, shaking his head in that peculiar way he had done since he was a lamb. When I scratched his cheek he'd close his eyes, chew the cud, and rub his head against my knee. Some days he'd walk with me to the beach, eating seaweed and sometimes even lying down next to me as I sat watching the comings and goings of birds, seals and otters.

When I'd told people that I was moving, their first question was what would happen to Yoda? Yoda had two available options, and as his owner I needed to make that decision for him. He had several offers of homes, where he'd be joining fields of contented caddies. Or the second option, and the one I chose, was for him to remain where he was, where he was happy, and where one day he would become mutton. I had spent so much of my research thinking about the interplay between concepts of autonomy, love and respect – what, then, would these mean for Yoda? For his future? Many pony breeders lamented relationships that infantilised animals, encouraging dependence and limiting opportunities. Although not cruel in a physical sense, this lack of respect for an animal's autonomy inhibits their natural behaviours, and can preclude the possibility of a human–animal relationship based on trust and mutual respect. In many ways, this parallelled how I felt about Yoda. None of the caddy fields felt appropriate. They all seemed very well cared for and happy but I knew these flocks didn't speak sheep. Would it be fair to limit Yoda's life in that way, even if it meant extending it? Could he be happy in a small square field when he currently had the freedom to wander across large stretches on hill and shore?

My four-day-old abandoned lamb with big eyes and knobbly knees who was terrified of sheep had, with time and love, learned to live with a flock. He rubbed cheeks and participated in mutual grooming, he engaged in play fights, and followed them to shelter behind the peat banks when the weather got stormy. He spent a lot of time with a group of six sheep that frequently left the main flock to go on their own adventures. I felt proud of him when I thought of what he had accomplished. How he had learned to become a sheep, and how, in many ways, this journey with Yoda had helped me to feel part of the community, connected through the shared experience of taking care of a caddy. I couldn't know for sure what he would choose but I did know he was healthy and happy and that I didn't want to take his hard-won independence away from him.

I knew Yoda would have several more years to live out on the ness before his day would come, and I know in many ways he is a very lucky sheep. After all, as a boy lamb bred for the UK meat industry, had he not been abandoned by his mum and become a bottle-fed pet, his time would have come in the autumn of his first year. When it is his time, I know exactly who will do the deed. I know they will be respectful and Yoda will not suffer. I also know that in many ways this is not death; it is the continuation of crofting life in this place. In autumn some of the yowes go to the ram, and the older wethers go to the freezer to make room for the new lambs that will arrive in spring. When Yoda's time comes his flesh will feed families who have kept sheep in this land for generations. The flock and family will continue to live together, their lives entwined together in this rugged and beautiful land.

On my last day on the island, as I watched the sea,

I noticed the detail of the rock I sat on: lichen-covered with long veins of quartz and a hint of golden sparkle – pyrite probably. On its weathered surface, from deep cracks, sea pinks grew. The grass surrounding me appeared green from a distance, but I knew that nestled between the blades of grass were tiny flowers with petals of yellow, blue and pink. Around me were the startled trills and pips of oystercatcher, distant, then closer as they circled overhead. My eyes traced the coastline, searching for what had startled them, hoping an otter might be nearby.

Suddenly, the sound of seal song rose from the water, joining sea and sky, connecting my body to the world. I felt the strong kicks of life inside me intensify. My baby, responding to the song of the sea. I wondered how it sounded to him. Was he responding to the seals, or to my reaction to them? How much did he understand about the world he would soon be part of? Was part of, I corrected myself, because he was there, part of me. Rohan, my baby boy. Named after the rowan tree, the timeless symbol of protection whose red berries signal a Scottish autumn. And that autumn, I would finally meet him.

ACKNOWLEDGEMENTS

I WOULD FIRST LIKE TO thank all the crofters, pony breeders, friends and neighbours who were part of my pony research. I was welcomed into people's homes and given the opportunity to spend time with their animals. The warmth and generosity of the people I met was truly overwhelming.

I was very lucky to do this research with ponies as a PhD student with Aberdeen University's Arctic Domus Project and I would particularly like to thank supervisors Prof. David Anderson and Dr. Robert Wishart for all their advice, support, patience and encouragement through the PhD process. Being part of such a project put me in touch with researchers working in some fascinating fields. Joining this group as a new PhD student, I expected such a gathering of academics to be intimidating however I could not have wished for a more welcoming and supportive group.

I am incredibly grateful for the support of my agent Jenny Brown for believing in this book from the very beginning and supporting me through the development and publication process. Thanks to my editor at Rider Bianca Bexton for her advice, support and encouragement and for making the journey to publication a really positive experience.

Huge thanks to my family, particularly my sons Rohan and Finn Mercer who joined me during this journey. You have filled each my days with excitement, joy and inspiration. Thank you to my husband Steve for all his support and for his willingness to join me on this adventure to Shetland. Thank you to my father Robin Munro for inspiring a love of books and reading from my earliest days and for taking such an interest in the work and offering advice and support, I would not have been able to do this without you. Also thanks to my mum Moyra Martineau for all her support and for her inspiring stories about the northern isles. I am also very grateful to the non-humans, particularly Sugar, Yukon and Yoda, who had such an impact on both my academic and personal life.